HAMLET: A GUIDE

The Shakespeare Handbooks

HAMLET

A Guide

ALISTAIR McCALLUM

Ivan R. Dee

CHICAGO

Library of Congress Cataloging-in-Publication Data:
McCallum, Alistair, 1954–
    Hamlet : a guide / Alistair McCallum.
      p. cm. — (The Shakespeare handbooks)
    ISBN 1-56663-358-3 (acid-free paper) — ISBN 1-56663-359-1 (pbk. :
acid-free paper)
    1. Shakespeare, William, 1564–1616. Hamlet—Handbooks, manuals, etc.
I. Title.

PR2807 .M325 2001
822.3'3—dc21
                                                            00-066030

Introduction

In many ways, the plays of Shakespeare's time had a great deal in common with the movie scripts of today. Their prime purpose was to entertain. They were often written to tight deadlines and frequently involved collaboration between writers. Constant revision, cutting and rewriting were the norm. Considerations such as the available actors, current political events, and the changing tastes of the public always had to be borne in mind. Particular productions might excite interest and controversy, but plays were regarded as ephemeral and were rarely published in book form. The poet or essayist might produce a slim, finely bound volume in the hope of literary immortality, but the playwright worked and lived firmly in the present. Plays had not yet become literature. Theatregoing was a pleasure, not a duty.

Four hundred years later, a great deal has changed. Shakespeare is no longer simply a popular playwright; he has become a symbol, an icon. His name generates enthusiasm and anxiety in equal measure. Competing armies of literary critics - a profession unknown in Shakespeare's day - are engaged in a ceaseless war over his reputation and the meaning of his work.

I was lucky enough to grow up in Stratford-on-Avon and, as a regular visitor to the Royal Shakespeare Theatre, became familiar with many of the plays. Whatever else Shakespeare might be, he was not intimidating. The mist surrounding the plays gradually cleared; structure, characters, and ideas started to emerge; the creative input of actors, directors and crew became apparent. The better I understood the plays, the more absorbing and meaningful they became. Familiarity certainly did not breed contempt.

Without this degree of familiarity, approaching a Shakespeare play can be a daunting business. Where do we look for help? There is certainly no shortage of excellent books that discuss, interpret, and analyze Shakespeare's work. But for most of us the problems in approaching Shakespeare are essentially practical: the complexity of his plots, compounded by the obscurity (to modern ears) of his language. What was entirely missing, it seemed to me, was something to guide readers through these difficulties and give them the confidence to respond freely to the plays. This is what I have attempted to provide with the *Shakespeare Handbooks*. Each book gives a straightforward, detailed account of the plot, scene by scene, with plenty of quotations from the play itself, and help with the more obscure words and phrases. I have also included a handful of comments from writers of diverse periods, backgrounds, and opinions, which I hope readers will find thought-provoking, and a few pertinent facts and figures relating to Shakespeare's life and times.

Of course there is no single correct interpretation of a Shakespeare play. His plays were scripts, after all, for his own acting company, a close-knit group of men who worked together for many years; he wrote no introductions or footnotes, and precious few stage directions. The scenery and costumes, the movements and interactions of characters, the mood of the play—all these aspects, and many more, will always be matters for the imaginative judgment of those staging the play. And above all, the creative responses of spectators and readers will be many, varied, and unpredictable.

Shakespeare is challenging. His plays are rich, profound, and enigmatic. The experience of staging, performing, watching or reading them should be a journey of exploration. I hope that the *Shakespeare Handbooks* will give my readers help and encouragement with the first few steps of that rewarding journey.

HAMLET: A GUIDE

Setting the scene

Shakespeare wrote *Hamlet* in or around 1600. He was in his mid-thirties, a successful dramatist and actor, and a member - and shareholder - of the most prestigious theatre company in London.

This was a prolific time in Shakespeare's career, particularly in the production of comedies; *Much Ado About Nothing, As You Like It* and *Twelfth Night* all date from this period. What prompted Shakespeare at this point in his life to turn to tragedy, a form he had so far handled lightly and infrequently, we can only guess. Whatever the motivation, the result was staggering; a vast, complex, disturbing drama, wildly imaginative in its plot and ravishing in its language. The play, which draws on ancient Norse legend for its central events, was an immediate and enduring success.

Hamlet occupies a central position in world literature. It has been translated into most of the world's languages, and over the centuries has provoked more comment, analysis and argument than any other single work of drama. It has been staged, filmed and televised more than any other Shakespearean play: in the first three decades of the twentieth century, the age of the silent movie, no fewer than seventeen film versions of *Hamlet* were made. The role of the Prince is regarded by many actors - and, for the last two hundred years, many actresses - as the greatest challenge of their careers.

And yet this play, Shakespeare's longest, so many of whose phrases have become a familiar part of the English language, remains, at heart, a mystery:

"Hamlet *is Shakespeare's most frequently performed play. Over the past four centuries of its rich and uninterrupted stage history, every generation has attempted to reinterpret the tragedy in terms of its own values and concerns. Audiences have been attracted to the drama not only because of the interpretive opportunities afforded by Shakespeare's provocatively ambiguous hero, but also because of the sheer beauty and insight of the poet's sublime verse . . . while most critics have acknowledged the impossibility of reconciling Hamlet's disparate, often conflicting traits into a coherent whole, performers and audiences continue to embrace the endeavour."*

Joseph C. Tardiff, *Shakespearean Criticism*, 1993

A death brings disquiet to Elsinore

Hamlet, King of Denmark, is dead. His brother Claudius has succeeded to the throne. Shortly after becoming King, Claudius married his brother's widow, Gertrude.

Prince Hamlet, son of the dead King, has returned from his studies at Wittenberg university to be present at the funeral of his father, and the coronation of his uncle; and, to his dismay, the unexpected remarriage of his mother.

At the royal court in Elsinore, Prince Hamlet's sullen, unpredictable behaviour is giving cause for concern. Meanwhile, a far more sinister development has been witnessed by the King's watchmen: in the depths of the night, the ghost of the old King, stern and warlike, has been seen marching in sombre silence outside the castle walls.

CURTAIN UP

A disturbing vision

I, i

In the dark, cold night, high on the walls of the King's castle at Elsinore, a lone sentry is keeping watch. Suddenly the silence is broken by a voice calling through the gloom. The sentry challenges the intruder: but then the approaching figure reveals himself as Barnardo, the officer due to take over on guard duty.

The sentry is grateful for the punctual arrival of his fellow-officer, revealing that he is troubled both in body and spirit:

Francisco	You come most carefully upon your hour.
Barnardo	'Tis now struck twelve. Get thee to bed, Francisco.
Francisco	For this relief much thanks. 'Tis bitter cold, And I am sick at heart.

As Francisco leaves, two others, Horatio and Marcellus, come to join Barnardo for the night watch. Their conversation immediately turns to the subject of the ghost that the two guards Barnardo and Marcellus have seen, during their watch, for the last two nights. Horatio is sceptical, believing that the ghost is nothing more than a product of his friends' imagination. For their part, Barnardo and Marcellus are determined to convince Horatio, a man of great learning, that they are telling the truth; they want him to see the ghost with his own eyes.

The discussion between Horatio and the two guards is interrupted as the ghost itself appears. Clad in royal armour, its resemblance to the dead King is beyond question. Horatio is shaken to the core, and for a few seconds is too terrified to speak. Urged on by the others, he raises the courage to address the spirit, and commands it to speak: but the ghost drifts silently away.

Horatio's scepticism has vanished, and the experience has left him profoundly uneasy. He is sure that the ghost's nightly appearance is, in some mysterious way, an omen of misfortune for the kingdom of Denmark.

Denmark prepares for conflict

Marcellus now raises another subject. He has noticed that there has been intense military activity in Denmark: weapons are flooding into the country, and shipbuilders are working day and night to strengthen the Danish fleet. Horatio reveals that there is currently a threat of invasion from Norway. He explains that old King Hamlet, whose ghost they have just seen, was once challenged to single combat by Fortinbras, King of Norway. King Hamlet defeated and killed the Norwegian King, and duly took possession of the land that Fortinbras had put at stake. Now young Fortinbras, Prince of Norway, is determined to regain the territory forfeited by his father, and has gathered together a band of warriors with the intention of invading Denmark: this, explains Horatio, is why such urgent military preparations are under way.

The ghost of the dead King now reappears. Horatio is determined to find out why the spirit has returned from the grave, and tries to communicate with it:

Horatio   I'll cross it though it blast me.¹ Stay, illusion:
        If thou hast any sound or use of voice,
        Speak to me.
        If there be any good thing to be done
        That may to thee do ease, and grace to me,
        Speak to me;
        If thou art privy to thy country's fate,
        Which, happily,² foreknowing may avoid,
        O speak . . .

    ¹ *I'll cross its path and confront it, even if it destroys me*
    ² *perhaps*

But the ghost still refuses to speak. When the cock crows, it starts to drift away: Horatio urges the guards to hold it back with their spears, but their efforts are in vain. Day is dawning, and the men reflect that the traditional belief that spirits must return to their graves at daybreak seems to be true. Returning to the castle, they decide that Prince Hamlet must be told about the ghost of his dead father.

"It is difficult to praise the poetry of Hamlet. *Nearly all the play is as familiar by often quotation as the New Testament. The great, wise, and wonderful beauty of the play is a part of the English mind for ever. It is difficult to live for a day anywhere in England (except in a theatre) without hearing or reading a part of* Hamlet.*"*

John Masefield, *William Shakespeare*, 1911

The new King addresses his subjects

I, ii

Claudius, King of Denmark, is holding court. Amongst those in attendance are Polonius, the King's chief adviser, and his son Laertes; Voltemand and Cornelius, two state officials; and, dressed all in black, the young Prince Hamlet, son of the dead King and nephew to Claudius. Accompanying Claudius is Gertrude, widow of the dead King and mother of the young Prince.

Addressing his subjects, Claudius is careful to emphasise the sadness that they have all felt at his brother's death. Nevertheless, he suggests, grieving for the dead must not allow the concerns of the living to be neglected:

King   Though yet of Hamlet our dear brother's death
               The memory be green,[1] and that it us befitted
               To bear our hearts in grief, and our whole
                   kingdom
               To be contracted in one brow of woe,
               Yet so far hath discretion fought with nature[2]
               That we with wisest sorrow think on him
               Together with remembrance of ourselves.

[1] *fresh, unfaded*
[2] *good sense and wisdom have struggled with*
our natural feelings of grief

The King refers diplomatically to his marriage to Gertrude, his sister-in-law, which took place shortly after King Hamlet's death:

King	Therefore our sometime sister, now our queen,
	Th'imperial jointress[1] to this warlike state,
	Have we, as 'twere with a defeated joy . . .
	With mirth in funeral and with dirge in
	marriage,
	In equal scale weighing delight and dole,
	Taken to wife.

[1] *heiress*

Claudius now raises the issue of Prince Fortinbras of Norway, and his desire to recover the lands forfeited by his father. He realises that, with the death of King Hamlet, Fortinbras may well consider this an opportune moment to launch an attack.

The present King of Norway, uncle of the young Prince Fortinbras, is old and bedridden, and knows little or nothing of his nephew's intentions. Claudius has decided to inform the King of Fortinbras's military preparations, emphasising that all the money, arms and manpower for his nephew's adventure are being supplied by the Norwegian state. Cornelius and Voltemand are dispatched to Norway to deliver the message to the King.

Now Claudius turns to Laertes, who has a request to make. The King assures the young man that he will always give generous consideration to any appeal from the son of his closest adviser. Laertes, who has been living in France for some time, explains that he was glad to come back to Denmark for the King's recent coronation; now, however, he wishes to return to France. Claudius, once he has established that Polonius has no objection to his son's departure, graciously grants him leave to return.

The Prince remains in mourning

The King's attention now turns to Prince Hamlet, the son of his dead brother. Both Claudius and Gertrude are concerned about Hamlet's continuing state of dejection. They urge him to come to terms with his father's death, to shake off his mood of despondency, and to abandon his black mourning clothes. Hamlet's response is cool and cryptic:

King	But now, my cousin Hamlet, and my son[1] -
Hamlet	A little more than kin, and less than kind.[2]
King	How is it that the clouds still hang on you?
Hamlet	Not so, my lord, I am too much in the sun.[3]
Queen	Good Hamlet, cast thy nighted colour off,
	And let thine eye look like a friend on Denmark.[4]
	Do not for ever with thy vailed lids
	Seek for thy noble father in the dust.
	Thou know'st 'tis common: all that lives must die,
	Passing through nature to eternity.

[1] *nephew, and now stepson*

[2] *we may be close relations, but there is no warmth between us, nor is there the likeness of father and son*

[3] *in the glare of public and royal attention; also, unhappy at the title 'son'*

[4] *your stepfather, the King*

Hamlet assures his mother that his grief is deep and genuine, in contrast, he hints, to the display of mourning that he has observed in court. Claudius becomes increasingly impatient, and his tone of sympathy changes as he launches into a thinly-veiled criticism of Hamlet's wilfulness:

King   'Tis sweet and commendable in your nature,
               Hamlet,
          To give these mourning duties to your father . . .
              . . . But to persever
          In obstinate condolement is a course
          Of impious stubbornness, 'tis unmanly grief,
          It shows a will most incorrect to heaven,
          A heart unfortified, a mind impatient . . .

The King emphasises that he wants Hamlet to think of him as a father, and announces that he considers Hamlet to be next in line to the throne of Denmark.

Hamlet has been studying at Wittenberg, and had intended to return there after his uncle's coronation: however, the King and his wife now make it clear that they want him to remain with them in Denmark. To their surprise, Hamlet acquiesces at once, without protest.

Claudius is delighted at Hamlet's unexpected obedience: every toast that he drinks today, he announces, will be accompanied by the thundering of cannons in celebration. He leaves in high spirits, followed by his Queen and courtiers.

Horatio brings alarming news

Hamlet remains behind in the empty state room. His grief over the death of his father, his loathing for his uncle, and his dismay at his mother's hasty remarriage have left him utterly desolate. He is overcome by a sense of pointlessness, and is even tempted by thoughts of suicide, although he knows it is forbidden by the Church:

Hamlet O that this too too sullied flesh would melt,
Thaw and resolve itself into a dew,
Or that the Everlasting had not fix'd
His canon[1] 'gainst self-slaughter. O God! God!
How weary, stale, flat, and unprofitable
Seem to me all the uses[2] of this world!
Fie on't, ah fie, 'tis an unweeded garden
That grows to seed; things rank and gross in
　　nature
Possess it merely.[3]

[1] *law*
[2] *customs, ways*
[3] *completely, utterly*

What disturbs Hamlet above all is the fact that his mother - who, like him, had loved the old King devotedly - has married so soon after the funeral. Her marriage to Claudius, whom Hamlet regards as gross, brutish and debauched, took place only a matter of weeks after King Hamlet's death.

While Hamlet is contemplating his mother's inexplicable weakness and inconstancy, Horatio approaches, along with the two guards, Barnardo and Marcellus, with whom he has just witnessed King Hamlet's ghost.

Horatio and Hamlet are old friends who have studied together at Wittenberg, and they greet each other warmly. Hamlet is keen to know what Horatio is doing in Denmark, and his answer provokes a spark of bitter humour from the Prince:

Hamlet	But what is your affair in Elsinore?
	We'll teach you to drink deep ere you depart.
Horatio	My lord, I came to see your father's funeral.
Hamlet	I prithee do not mock me, fellow-student.
	I think it was to see my mother's wedding.
Horatio	Indeed, my lord, it follow'd hard upon.
Hamlet	Thrift, thrift, Horatio. The funeral bak'd meats
	Did coldly furnish forth the marriage tables.

The conversation turns to the subject of Hamlet's father. Horatio cautiously breaks the news of the previous night's events to his friend:

Horatio	I saw him once; a[1] was a goodly king.
Hamlet	A was a man, take him for all in all:
	I shall not look upon his like again.
Horatio	My lord, I think I saw him yesternight.

[1] *he*

Hamlet immediately demands to know more, and Horatio relates the full story of the previous night's watch, describing how the armed figure had marched slowly and silently past the three of them out on the castle battlements.

Eager to learn every last detail of the episode, Hamlet questions the men closely. Eventually he decides to join them on their watch: if the spirit appears again, and is indeed the ghost of his father, he resolves to speak to it. Urging them to keep their experience absolutely secret, he agrees to meet Horatio and the guards tonight on the castle walls.

Although he is impatient to confront and question the ghost, Hamlet is uneasy. He suspects that its appearance may be a token of some dreadful crime that has not yet come to light:

Hamlet   My father's spirit - in arms! All is not well.
I doubt[1] some foul play. Would the night were
   come.
Till then sit still, my soul. Foul deeds will rise,
Though[2] all the earth o'erwhelm them, to men's
   eyes.

[1] *fear, suspect*
[2] *even if*

Some stern words for Ophelia

I, iii

Laertes, his request to return to France granted by the King, is about to set off on his journey. He is bidding a fond farewell to his sister Ophelia, and urges her to write to him at every opportunity.

Ophelia has been spending a great deal of time with Prince Hamlet lately, and his affection for her is clear. Laertes warns his sister not to take Hamlet's attentions seriously; he is young and impulsive, and his feelings for her will soon change. Besides, explains Laertes, as heir to the throne Hamlet is not free to choose his future wife, so she must not put too much faith in any promises he makes. Laertes urges Ophelia to keep any feelings of affection or desire for the Prince strictly under control, and to stay well away from temptation.

Ophelia is disappointed to hear that Hamlet's love is likely to prove short-lived. She promises to remember her brother's advice, but hopes that he too will be restrained and virtuous in his conduct:

Ophelia   . . . good my brother,
            Do not as some ungracious pastors do,
            Show me the steep and thorny way to heaven,
            Whiles like a puff'd[1] and reckless libertine
            Himself the primrose path of dalliance[2] treads,
            And recks not his own rede.[3]

[1] *proud*
[2] *the path of amorous pleasure, leading to damnation*
[3] *takes no heed of his own warnings*

Polonius now comes in, telling his son to make haste; his ship is ready to depart. However, he wishes to offer a few words of advice to the young man before he sets off on his travels. Despite the hurry, Polonius takes his time, and his few words develop into a lengthy and wide-ranging lecture:

Polonius   Give every man thy ear, but few thy voice;
                 Take each man's censure, but reserve thy judgment.
                 . . . Neither a borrower nor a lender be,
                 For loan oft loses both itself and friend,
                 And borrowing dulls the edge of husbandry.[1]
                 This above all: to thine own self be true,
                 And it must follow as the night the day
                 Thou canst not then be false to any man.

    [1] *thrift*

Finally Laertes takes his leave, telling Ophelia to remember his advice. Polonius is curious: when Laertes has gone, he asks his daughter what advice he was referring to. When Ophelia tells him that it concerned Hamlet, Polonius is glad; he has been worried recently that she has been spending too much time alone with the Prince, and welcomes this opportunity to discuss the matter. Like Laertes, Polonius is deeply uneasy about the close relationship developing between Ophelia and the Prince. Hamlet's declarations of love are worthless, he maintains:

"Ophelia's modest Replies, the few Words she uses, and the virtuous Caution she gives her Brother after his Advice to her are inimitably charming. This I have observed in general in our Author's Plays, that almost all his young Women . . . are made to behave with a Modesty and Decency peculiar to those Times, and which are of such pleasing Simplicity as seem too ignorant and unmeaning in our well taught, knowing Age . . ."

George Stubbes, *Some Remarks on the Tragedy of Hamlet*, 1736

Polonius	What is between you? Give me up the truth.
Ophelia	He hath, my lord, of late made many tenders[1]
	Of his affection to me.
Polonius	Affection? Pooh, you speak like a green girl,
	Unsifted[2] in such perilous circumstance.
	Do you believe his tenders, as you call them?
Ophelia	I do not know, my lord, what I should think.
Polonius	Marry, I will teach you. Think yourself a baby
	That you have ta'en these tenders for true pay
	Which are not sterling.[3]

[1] *expressions; offers*
[2] *inexperienced*
[3] *not valid currency*

Ophelia insists that Hamlet has so far been both sincere and honourable, but Polonius refuses to change his mind. In fact the more he talks about the young man's fickleness, the more he convinces himself that Hamlet's real aim is nothing more than a brief sexual conquest. Finally he orders his daughter to stay away from the Prince entirely. Ophelia promises to obey.

The ghost summons Hamlet

I, iv

It is midnight. Hamlet has joined Horatio and Marcellus on the platform, high up on the castle walls, where the ghost has appeared for the last three nights.

The sound of cannon-fire suddenly bursts through the cold night air. Horatio is alarmed, but Hamlet explains that the King is indulging in a late-night drinking spree, and is ordering cannons to be fired to accompany his toasts. It is a tradition in Denmark, he says, although not one that is frequently observed:

Hamlet   . . . as he drains his draughts of Rhenish[1] down,
               The kettle-drum and trumpet[2] thus bray out
               The triumph of his pledge.
Horatio   Is it a custom?
Hamlet   Ay marry is't,
               But to my mind, though I am native here
               And to the manner born, it is a custom
               More honour'd in the breach[3] than the
                  observance.

[1] *wine*
[2] *signals for the cannon to fire*
[3] *by being ignored, overlooked*

Hamlet reflects sadly on the widespread drunkenness, typified in his uncle, that gives his country such a bad reputation. Other nations associate the Danes with heavy drinking, and disregard their achievements, just as an individual's good qualities can be tainted by some particular flaw in his character.

The Prince is suddenly shaken out of his contemplation by the arrival of the ghost. He immediately decides to question the armed figure, desperate to know why his father's spirit has come back from the dead. The ghost does not speak, but beckons Hamlet to leave his companions and follow him away from the platform.

Horatio and Marcellus urge Hamlet not to follow the ghost, fearing that it may be an evil spirit that will lead him into danger or madness. Hamlet remains unmoved by their warnings. He is determined to speak with the ghost, and his safety is of no importance. The others try to hold him back, but he fights them off and resolutely sets off into the night after the ghost.

Horatio and Marcellus hesitate for a moment, unsure whether to respect the Prince's wish to be left alone. They decide to follow him, convinced that he is in peril. They are sure that these frightening events do not bode well for the nation:

Horatio	He waxes[1] desperate with imagination.
Marcellus	Let's follow. 'Tis not fit thus to obey him.
Horatio	Have after. To what issue will this come?
Marcellus	Something is rotten in the state of Denmark.

[1] *grows, becomes*

The first performances of *Hamlet* were probably at the Globe theatre, on the south bank of the Thames, in 1600 or 1601.

Some years later, an amateur production was staged, thousands of miles away, in very different circumstances. It was presented on board the *Dragon*, a ship of the recently-formed East India Company, anchored off Sierra Leone. We can only guess at what props, costumes and scenery, if any, were available. The official journal entry of the captain, William Keeling, disguises the fact that he was a great amateur dramatics enthusiast and Shakespeare aficionado who organised the performance (and several subsequent ones) himself:

1608, Mar. 31. I envited Captain Hawkins to a ffishe dinner, and had Hamlet *acted abord me: which I permitt to keepe my people from idleness and unlawful games, or sleepe.*

The truth emerges

I, v

Hamlet, following the ghost through the darkness, appeals to it to speak. Urging him to listen carefully, the ghost reveals that he is indeed the spirit of the old King, destined to suffer in Purgatory until his sins are expiated:

Ghost	I am thy father's spirit,
	Doom'd for a certain term to walk the night,
	And for the day confin'd to fast in fires,
	Till the foul crimes done in my days of nature
	Are burnt and purg'd away.

It was believed by everyone, including the Prince, that King Hamlet died from a snakebite while sleeping in his orchard. The ghost now reveals the truth. His death was no accident:

Ghost	If thou didst ever thy dear father love -
Hamlet	O God!
Ghost	Revenge his foul and most unnatural murder.
Hamlet	Murder!
Ghost	Murder most foul, as in the best it is . . .
	. . . know, thou noble youth,
	The serpent that did sting thy father's life
	Now wears his crown.

Hamlet is devastated. His uncle, driven by lust for power and for his brother's wife, has committed murder: not only has he escaped punishment, but he is enjoying the fruits of his wrongdoing to the full. And the Queen, who had seemed almost to idolise her husband, allowed herself, after his death, to be seduced by the brutish Claudius.

The spirit of the King now discloses the manner of his death. While he was asleep in his orchard one afternoon, his brother

Claudius had crept up to him and poured a phial of deadly poison into his ear. The poison spread swiftly through the King's body, and he died soon afterwards, covered in foul scales and blisters. Deprived of the chance to pray or to be absolved of his sins, the King has been suffering in Purgatory since his death. The ghost implores Hamlet to take revenge on Claudius: as for Queen Gertrude, she should not be harmed, but must be allowed to suffer the pangs of her own conscience.

Daybreak is approaching, and the ghost disappears. Hamlet, overwhelmed by what he has seen and heard, resolves to make his dead father's wish the sole aim of his life from this moment on. All the learning of his student days must be erased, to be replaced with the dreadful knowledge of his uncle's treachery and the determination to avenge his father's death. As a symbol of his resolve, he commits this new-found truth to paper:

Hamlet   Yea, from the table[1] of my memory
             I'll wipe away all trivial fond records,
             All saws[2] of books, all forms, all pressures past . . .
                          Meet[3] it is I set it down
             That one may smile, and smile, and be a
                 villain -
             At least I am sure it may be so in Denmark.
                 [*Writes.*]

             [1] *writing-tablet*
             [2] *sayings, proverbs*
             [3] *fitting, appropriate*

Revenge was a popular theme in Elizabethan theatre, and tumultuous, bloody, and spectacular dramas on this theme attracted large audiences. Shakespeare rarely gave revenge a central position in his plays, with the notable exception of *Hamlet*, where its treatment is far more complex than in most dramas of the time. The morality of taking revenge for a serious crime such as murder was a hotly debated issue. Church and State remained firmly against private acts of revenge, and the Bible was often quoted in this context:

"Recompense to no man evil for evil . . . as much as lieth in you, live peaceably with all men. Dearly beloved, avenge not yourselves, but rather give place unto wrath: for it is written, Vengeance is mine; I will repay, saith the Lord."

Letter of Saint Paul to the Romans, King James Bible, 1611

The witnesses are sworn to secrecy

Horatio and Marcellus, who have been trying to find Hamlet, now catch up with him. They are relieved to see that he is safe, and are curious to know what he has learnt from the ghost.

With the discovery of the truth about his father's death, and his new-found sense of purpose, Hamlet's mood has changed dramatically. He is suddenly high-spirited and playful, and his friends are baffled by his whimsical, irrational words. He assures them that the ghost was truly the spirit of his dead father, but refuses to tell them what it has divulged.

Hamlet asks his companions to swear that they will never reveal their knowledge of the ghost to anyone else. They consent readily, but Hamlet asks them to swear again, this time on the cross of his sword; and the voice of the ghost, calling from beneath the ground, commands them to do the same. As they are about to give their oath, the ghost's voice is heard a second time, from a different spot under the ground. Hamlet, still light-hearted, takes his friends to the site of the voice and tries again:

Hamlet	. . . we'll shift our ground.
	Come hither, gentlemen,
	And lay your hands again upon my sword.
	Swear by my sword
	Never to speak of this that you have heard.
Ghost	Swear by his sword. [*They swear.*]
Hamlet	Well said, old mole. Canst work i'th' earth so fast?
	A worthy pioner!¹

¹ *digger, miner*

Horatio is amazed by the ghost and its ability to move around freely under the earth. Hamlet, convinced that there is a world of phenomena beyond the limits of human knowledge, suggests that Horatio should accept the experience gladly:

Shakespeare was, unusually for his time, an actor as well as a playwright. However, about his acting almost nothing is known. Whether he gave up acting at an early stage in favour of playwriting, what types of roles he undertook, how gifted he was as an actor, are all questions that must remain unanswered. One of the first Shakespearean scholars, writing nearly a century after his death, offers a tantalising but ambiguous detail:

". . . *tho' I have inquir'd, I could never meet with any further Account of him in this way, than that the top of his Performance was the Ghost in his own Hamlet.*"

Nicholas Rowe, Introduction to *Works of Shakespeare*, 1709

Horatio	O day and night, but this is wondrous strange.
Hamlet	And therefore as a stranger give it welcome.
	There are more things in heaven and earth,
	Horatio,
	Than are dreamt of in your philosophy.

The Prince now discloses another secret. From now on, he warns, his behaviour may be deliberately bizarre, even to the point of apparent madness. He refuses to tell his two friends why this may be necessary, but he insists that they do not give the slightest hint to anyone that his mental disturbance is a pretence. Again the voice of the dead King resounds from under the earth, and Horatio and Marcellus swear that they will keep the secret.

Calmer and more sombre now, Hamlet asks his companions to return to the castle with him. The responsibility of his knowledge is already starting to weigh heavily upon him:

Hamlet	The time is out of joint.[1] O cursed spite,
	That ever I was born to set it right.

[1] *dislocated, disordered*

A secret mission for Reynaldo

II, i

Polonius is about to dispatch his servant Reynaldo to Paris, to visit his son Laertes. He gives Reynaldo some money and some letters to hand to his son, and asks him to make discreet but thorough enquiries regarding the young man's behaviour. The method by which Reynaldo is to gain this information is devious in the extreme, and Polonius's instructions are lengthy and detailed to the point of absurdity:

Polonius   . . . Inquire me[1] first what Danskers[2] are in Paris,
And how, and who, what means, and where they
   keep,[3]
What company, at what expense . . .

[1] *for me*
[2] *Danes*
[3] *what money they live on, where their lodgings are*

Reynaldo must pretend not to know Laertes well. However, continues Polonius, he must claim to know of the young man's infamous reputation, being careful to put it down to youthful high spirits rather than bad character. Reynaldo becomes confused, as Polonius's idea of normal conduct in young men differs widely from his own:

Polonius	. . . put on him[1]
	What forgeries you please - marry, none so rank
	As may dishonour him - take heed of that -
	But, sir, such wanton, wild, and usual slips
	As are companions noted and most known
	To youth and liberty.
Reynaldo	As gaming, my lord?
Polonius	Ay, or drinking, fencing, swearing,
	Quarrelling, drabbing[2] - you may go so far.
Reynaldo	My lord, that would dishonour him.
Polonius	'Faith no, as you may season it in the charge.[3]

[1] *attribute to him*
[2] *visiting brothels*
[3] *not if you word your accusations carefully*

Reynaldo asks his master why he should go to such lengths, charging his son with this catalogue of misdemeanours. Polonius proudly reveals the thinking behind his plan. If there is the slightest element of truth in the allegations, he explains, it is bound to emerge in the course of Reynaldo's conversations. Whoever he is talking to will surely have no reservations about revealing anything that confirms the general picture that Reynaldo will have painted. In other circumstances people might feel reticent about giving away such details, but Reynaldo's false accusations will encourage the disclosure of truths about Laertes that might otherwise remain hidden:

Polonius	. . . Your bait of falsehood takes this carp of truth;
	And thus do we of wisdom and of reach,[1]
	With windlasses and with assays of bias,[2]
	By indirections find directions out.

[1] *those of us who have wisdom and understanding*
[2] *in roundabout ways, and with devious tests*

Although Polonius is keen to know the truth about Laertes, he tells his servant to make sure his investigations are kept secret from his son. With a final injunction to allow Laertes the freedom to enjoy his pastimes, whatever they may be, he sends Reynaldo on his way.

. . . By indirections find directions out. '

Polonius compares his devious method of finding the truth to the playing of bowls. The 'bias' - a bulge or weight in one side of the bowl, which causes it to follow a curved path - means that the player must aim away from the target, not directly at it.

Shakespeare uses images drawn from bowls so frequently that at least one scholar has concluded that it was his favourite sport:

"Of all the games and exercises Shakespeare mentions - tennis, football, bowls, fencing, tilting, wrestling - there can be no doubt that bowls was the one he himself played and loved best. He has nineteen images from bowls, or more than thrice as many as from any other game . . ."

Caroline Spurgeon, *Shakespeare's Imagery and What It Tells Us,* 1935

Hamlet is behaving strangely

Ophelia now comes in, in a state of agitation, to talk to her father. She reports that she has just had a distressing visit from Prince Hamlet:

Ophelia ... Pale as his shirt, his knees knocking each other,
And with a look so piteous in purport
As if he had been loosed out of hell
To speak of horrors, he comes before me.

Polonius does not have a moment's doubt. There can only be one explanation: the Prince has been driven mad by love for his daughter. During his visit, says Ophelia, Hamlet did not speak; he just held her tightly by the wrist and gazed at her face intently. Eventually he gave a forlorn sigh and left, his eyes fixed on her to the last.

Convinced that Hamlet, in his madness, is likely to come to harm or even take his own life, Polonius decides to speak to King Claudius at once. He asks his daughter whether she has spoken harshly to the Prince recently; she replies that she has avoided all contact with him, just as Polonius himself had instructed. She has even sent back his letters.

Polonius concludes, remorsefully, that Hamlet's insanity is his fault. He had misjudged the Prince's feelings, he realises, reflecting that the old are as likely to make mistakes through being too wary as the young are through their impulsiveness. To hide the truth about Hamlet's madness would only make matters worse, decides Polonius. He sets off to see the King at once, to confess how his actions have led to the Prince's disturbed state of mind.

Good news from Norway

II, ii

Rosencrantz and Guildenstern, two old friends of Hamlet's, have been summoned to the King's presence. Claudius explains that the Prince seems to have undergone a dreadful change recently: apart from the death of the old King, he has no idea what has provoked it. He hopes that Hamlet's two friends may be able to shed some light on the cause of the young man's disorder. The Queen, equally anxious to find out what is afflicting her son, asks Rosencrantz and Guildenstern to remain at court until some improvement in Hamlet's condition can be achieved. She reassures them that they will be richly rewarded.

Both men declare themselves more than willing to help, and gladly put themselves at the monarchs' disposal. They are led off immediately to see the Prince.

Polonius now enters, announcing that Voltemand and Cornelius, the two officials sent to visit the King of Norway, have returned. They bring good news, he assures the King, and so does he; he is confident that he has pinpointed the cause of Hamlet's derangement.

The King is delighted, and is impatient to hear what Polonius has discovered. However, the returning ambassadors must first be received. As Polonius goes to bring them in, the King excitedly breaks the news to his wife. She does not share his faith in Polonius's judgement, and fears that the cause of the problem is all too clear:

King	He tells me, my dear Gertrude, he hath found
	The head and source of all your son's distemper.
Queen	I doubt[1] it is no other but the main,[2]
	His father's death and our o'er-hasty marriage.

[1] *suspect, fear*
[2] *the prominent, obvious reason*

Polonius returns with the ambassadors. Voltemand reports that the Norwegian King was shocked to hear of the military expedition planned by his nephew Fortinbras. He had indeed been aware that troops were being assembled, but had been misled into believing that the objective was an assault on their enemy Poland, not on Denmark. Angry at this attempt to take advantage of his age and infirmity, the King had immediately ordered the military preparations to be brought to a halt. Fortinbras then appeared before the King to give his word that he would never again enter into hostilities against Denmark.

The Norwegian King, pleased with Fortinbras's prompt response, has given him permission to use his assembled troops to capture land from Poland. However, this will involve the movement of troops across Danish territory, so Claudius's permission will clearly be required. The letter requesting this permission is now handed to Claudius, who is very satisfied with the outcome. The threat of invasion has been averted, and the King of Norway is now in his debt; there will be feasting and drinking tonight, he promises.

Polonius puts forward his theory

Polonius now returns to the question of the Prince. He indulges in a lengthy, rambling introduction to his subject-matter:

Polonius   My liege and madam, to expostulate
What majesty should be, what duty is,
Why day is day, night night, and time is time,
Were nothing but to waste night, day, and time.
Therefore, since brevity is the soul of wit,
And tediousness the limbs and outward flourishes,
I will be brief.

> *"Polonius is a man bred in courts, exercised in business, stored with observation, confident of his knowledge, proud of his eloquence, and declining into dotage . . . Such a man is positive and confident, because he knows that his mind was once strong, and knows not that it has become weak. Such a man excels in general principles, but fails in the particular application. He is knowing in retrospect, and ignorant in foresight."*
>
> Dr Johnson, in his edition of *The Plays of William Shakespeare*, 1765

The Queen soon tires of Polonius's verbiage, and urges him to abandon his rhetoric. Finally he comes to the point. He has a letter, written by Hamlet to Ophelia, and dutifully passed on to him by his daughter. It is a love-letter, full of ardent expressions of devotion, including a brief poem:

> *Doubt thou the stars are fire,*
> *Doubt that the sun doth move,*
> *Doubt[1] truth to be a liar,*
> *But never doubt I love.*
> *O dear Ophelia, I am ill at these numbers.[2] I have not*
> *art to reckon my groans.[3] But that I love thee best, O*
> *most best, believe it. Adieu.*
> *Thine evermore . . .*
> > *Hamlet.*

[1] *suspect*
[2] *bad at writing verse*
[3] *to count or to express my sighs*

Polonius admits that he intervened when he became aware of the romance, although he is keen to stress that he believed he was doing the right thing. He commanded Ophelia to have nothing to do with the Prince, he explains, whose station in life is so far above her own. She obeyed, with terrible consequences:

Polonius   . . . she took the fruits of my advice,
             And he, repelled - a short tale to make -
             Fell into a sadness, then into a fast,
             Thence to a watch,[1] thence into a weakness,
             Thence to a lightness,[2] and, by this declension,
             Into the madness wherein now he raves
             And all we mourn for.

             [1] *wakefulness, insomnia*
             [2] *delirium*

Claudius and Gertrude agree that the explanation is highly convincing. Polonius, certain that he is on the right track, proposes to test his theory. He suggests that they should arrange for Hamlet and Ophelia to meet while he and the King hide behind a screen and eavesdrop on their conversation. He is confident that this will reveal the true cause of the Prince's madness. The King decides to go along with the plan.

> "*The first edition of Shakespeare's tragedy,* Hamlet, *and the first part of Cervantes'* Don Quixote *appeared in the same year at the very beginning of the seventeenth century. This coincidence seems to me significant . . . It seems to me that in these two types are embodied two opposite fundamental peculiarities of man's nature - the two ends of the axis about which it turns. I think that all people belong, more or less, to one of these two types. In our day, it is true, the Hamlets have become far more numerous than the Don Quixotes . . .*"
>
> Ivan Turgenev, *Hamlet and Don Quixote,* 1860

Hamlet now enters, apparently absorbed in a book. Polonius asks Claudius and Gertrude to leave him on his own with the Prince. They go, and Polonius attempts to engage the young man in conversation. He is baffled by the Prince's answers, although he remains convinced that it is his passion for Ophelia that has brought about his confusion. Indeed, he even believes he recognises the signs of unrequited love:

Hamlet	. . . Have you a daughter?
Polonius	I have, my lord.
Hamlet	Let her not walk i'th' sun.[1] Conception[2] is a blessing, but as your daughter may conceive - friend, look to't.
Polonius	[*aside*] How say you by that?[3] Still harping on my daughter . . . truly in my youth I suffered much extremity for love, very near this.

[1] *be too much in the public eye; become warm and fertile*
[2] *understanding*
[3] *that proves my point*

Trying a different tack, Polonius asks Hamlet what he is reading. Again his words are puzzling, although Polonius detects an element of sense in his replies:

Polonius	What do you read, my lord?
Hamlet	Words, words, words.
Polonius	What is the matter, my lord?
Hamlet	Between who?
Polonius	I mean the matter that you read, my lord.
Hamlet	Slanders, sir. For the satirical rogue says here that old men have gray beards, that their faces are wrinkled . . . all which, sir, though I most powerfully and potently

| | believe, yet I hold it not honesty to have it thus set down. For yourself, sir, shall grow old as I am - if like a crab you could go backward. |
| Polonius | [aside] Though this be madness, yet there is method in't. |

Polonius takes his leave. Hamlet, making no attempt to hide his antipathy towards the old man, urges him to be on his way.

Hamlet's melancholy is revealed

Rosencrantz and Guildenstern, sent by the King to learn more about Hamlet's state of mind, now join him. Hamlet is pleased to see his old friends, and is curious to know what has brought them to the court at Elsinore. For himself, he declares, he feels like a prisoner, although he acknowledges that the feeling springs from his own imagination:

Hamlet	What have you, my good friends, deserved at the hands of Fortune that she sends you to prison hither?
Guildenstern	Prison, my lord?
Hamlet	Denmark's a prison.
Rosencrantz	Then is the world one.
Hamlet	A goodly one, in which there are many confines, wards, and dungeons, Denmark being one o'th' worst.
Rosencrantz	We think not so, my lord.
Hamlet	Why, then 'tis none to you; for there is nothing either good or bad but thinking makes it so. To me it is a prison.

Hamlet returns to the subject of the reason for their visit. He
has an inkling that the King has sent for them; unable to make a
direct denial, his two friends eventually admit that his suspicion
is justified. However, Hamlet is not angry with them. He is
aware that his mother and stepfather are trying to discover the
cause of the recent change in his behaviour, and he reveals to his
friends the depths of the depression into which he has sunk. He
has lost interest in life, and the beauty and splendour of the world
have disappeared, leaving squalor and decay in their place:

Hamlet   I have of late, but wherefore I know not, lost all
                my mirth, forgone all custom of exercises; and
                indeed it goes so heavily with my disposition
                that this goodly frame[1] the earth seems to me a
                sterile promontory, this most excellent canopy
                the air, look you, this brave o'erhanging
                firmament, this majestical roof fretted with
                golden fire,[2] why, it appeareth nothing to me but
                a foul and pestilent congregation of vapours.

[1] *structure*
[2] *adorned with stars*

---

*"This play has a prophetic truth, which is above that of his-
tory. Whoever has become thoughtful and melancholy through
his own mishaps or those of others . . . whose powers of action
have been eaten up by thought, he to whom the universe seems
infinite, and himself nothing; whose bitterness of soul makes
him careless of consequences . . . this is the true Hamlet."*

William Hazlitt, *Characters of Shakespear's Plays*, 1817

Humanity, too, seems to him to have lost all its greatness and nobility, and to be worthless and insignificant:

Hamlet   What a piece of work is a man, how noble
in reason, how infinite in faculties, in form
and moving how express and admirable, in
action how like an angel, in apprehension[1]
how like a god: the beauty of the world, the
paragon of animals - and yet, to me, what is
this quintessence of dust? Man delights
not me . . .

[1] *insight, intelligence, reasoning*

A new development in the theatre

Rosencrantz mentions that a troupe of actors is visiting the court. Hamlet is a great devotee of the stage, and his curiosity is immediately aroused. He is surprised to learn that the visiting players are those of the capital's principal company; they are normally resident at their playhouse in the city. Rosencrantz hints that there is a ban on performances at the playhouses at the moment because of political unrest.

To make matters worse, a new company of boy actors, playing in a private theatre, has suddenly shot to fame. The traditional public playhouses, and their writers, are suffering as a result:

Rosencrantz   . . . there is, sir, an eyrie of children, little eyases,[1]
that cry out on the top of question,[2] and are
most tyrannically clapped for't. These are now
the fashion, and so berattle[3] the common stages -
so they call them - that many wearing rapiers are
afraid of goose-quills and dare scarce come thither.[4]

[1] *noisy young hawks*
[2] *screech out their lines at the top of their voices*
[3] *condemn, disparage*
[4] *men of fashion will not set foot in the public
playhouses for fear of ridicule*

Hamlet is dismayed to hear that the old playhouses have
fallen out of favour so quickly. He reflects on the ease with which
public opinion changes; those who used to loathe his uncle in the
days of King Hamlet idolise him now that he is in power.

. . . an eyrie of children, little eyases . . .

This reference to contemporary theatrical events is unique in Shakespeare. Children's acting companies, made up of schoolboys or choirboys and presenting light courtly entertainment, often in Latin, had been very popular in royal circles as early as 1520. Their popularity waned with the rise of professional adult companies and public theatres later in the century.

However, the children's companies enjoyed a major revival around 1600 as their directors started to offer more ambitious, controversial plays, often with a strong political content, by authors such as Ben Jonson. In addition, their performances were generally indoors, in expensive, intimate, candlelit theatres, as opposed to the large public playhouses such as the Globe which were open to the elements and which held performances by daylight.

Theatrical in-fighting - with rivalry between the various children's companies, between the children's companies and the adult companies, and most of all between individual playwrights - was at its height at the time of *Hamlet*. Many plays of the time are full of ridicule, scathing caricatures, and bitter personal attacks and counter-attacks. During this conflict - known at the time as the 'War of the Poets', and probably fuelled by a desire for publicity as well as by genuine resentment - Shakespeare seems to have kept at a safe distance.

Hamlet welcomes the players

A sudden blast of trumpets heralds the arrival of the players. Hamlet realises that, with all his questioning and musing, he has hardly given his friends a proper welcome. He assures them now that he is indeed happy to see them again, and suggests cryptically that he may be more sane than the King and Queen believe. He can still make the distinctions that matter - for example, between a hunter's bird of prey and an innocent tool:

Hamlet	Gentlemen, you are welcome to Elsinore. Your hands, come then . . . But my uncle-father and aunt-mother are deceived.
Guildenstern	In what, my dear lord?
Hamlet	I am but mad north-north-west. When the wind is southerly, I know a hawk from a handsaw.

Polonius now arrives to introduce the actors. He is enthusiastic about both their powers and their versatility:

Polonius	The best actors in the world, either for tragedy, comedy, history, pastoral, pastoral-comical, historical-pastoral, tragical-historical, tragical-comical-historical-pastoral, scene individable,[1] or poem unlimited. Seneca[2] cannot be too heavy, nor Plautus[2] too light.

> [1] *play that cannot be put into any category*
> [2] *the most renowned tragic and comic playwrights, respectively, of ancient Rome*

Hamlet teases Polonius, singing a few lines of a ballad about Jephthah, a warrior of ancient Israel forced to sacrifice his only daughter in fulfilment of a reckless promise. Polonius, baffled by Hamlet's train of thought, concludes that he is still obsessed with Ophelia.

The players now enter. Hamlet knows them well, and greets them cordially. There have been a few changes since he last saw them, and the young boy who plays the female roles has grown. Hamlet hopes that his voice has not broken:

Hamlet   ... What, my young lady and mistress! By'r lady, your ladyship is nearer to heaven than when I saw you last by the altitude of a chopine.[1] Pray God your voice, like a piece of uncurrent gold, be not cracked within the ring.[2]

[1] *a high-soled shoe*
[2] *rendered worthless, like a gold coin whose edges have been clipped*

In the company of the players, Hamlet is in his element. He quickly becomes animated and talkative, and calls for an impromptu performance. He remembers a speech that he had found particularly striking, although he recalls that the play in which it was spoken had not proved a success with the public:

Hamlet   ... the play, I remember, pleased not the million, 'twas caviare to the general.[1] But it was, as I received it - and others, whose judgments in such matters cried in the top of mine[2] - an excellent play ...

[1] *rare and special, not appreciated by the majority*
[2] *had far more authority than mine*

Remembering the point in the story at which his favourite speech occurred, Hamlet struggles to think of the first line. It finally comes back to him: but instead of letting the players continue, the Prince becomes carried away and launches into a dramatic recital himself. After a dozen lines he stops to allow one of the players to complete the passage.

The subject of the speech is the fall of Troy. It describes the murder of King Priam by the vengeful Pyrrhus, and the distraught lamenting of Priam's wife Hecuba. At the end of his speech the player, describing Hecuba's grief, seems to be on the verge of tears himself. His listeners are moved. Hamlet, full of admiration, emphasises to Polonius that the actors must be treated with the utmost consideration during their stay in court:

Hamlet	Good my lord, will you see the players well bestowed?[1] Do you hear, let them be well used, for they are the abstract and brief chronicles of the time . . .
Polonius	My lord, I will use them according to their desert.[2]
Hamlet	God's bodkin, man, much better. Use every man after his desert, and who shall scape whipping?

[1] *given good accommodation*
[2] *treat them as well as they deserve*

"*Players, said Hamlet, are the abstract and brief chronicles of the time. That was also the view of Queen Elizabeth; and the history of the theatres shows that every few months a sensitive Government peremptorily commanded them to be shut . . . In 1603, when the Queen was dying, the first step taken to guard against disorder was to shut the playhouses.*"

G. B. Harrison, *Introducing Shakespeare*, 1966

A plan to reveal the King's guilt

As Polonius leads the troupe away, Hamlet takes the chief player aside for a private word. He asks whether the company can perform a play entitled 'The Murder of Gonzago' tomorrow evening: the player confirms that they know the piece.

Hamlet then asks him whether he can quickly learn an additional speech, which Hamlet will supply himself, and include it in the performance. The player agrees, and goes off to join the rest of the company.

Rosencrantz and Guildenstern leave too, and Hamlet is on his own. He is suddenly overcome with bitter self-loathing. The player's anguish over the imagined events in ancient Troy puts to shame his own reaction to his father's murder. He should have taken swift action in revenge, he tells himself:

Hamlet   O what a rogue and peasant slave am I!
Is it not monstrous that this player here,
But in a fiction, in a dream of passion,
Could force his soul so to his own conceit[1]
That from her working all his visage wann'd,
Tears in his eyes . . .
                  . . . ere this
I should ha' fatted all the region kites[2]
With this slave's offal. Bloody, bawdy villain!
Remorseless, treacherous, lecherous, kindless[3]
    villain!

[1] *to the emotion that he considers fitting*
[2] *the scavenging hawks of the air*
[3] *unnatural*

Cursing himself for continually taking refuge in language, Hamlet decides that he must act. However, before he takes revenge, he wants to be absolutely sure of his uncle's guilt. Perhaps the ghost was sent by the devil to trick him; in his state of melancholy, he realises, he may be susceptible to delusions.

The lines Hamlet intends to insert in the forthcoming play will prove the truth one way or the other; for they describe, in the guise of fiction, the murder of King Hamlet. Claudius's reaction on seeing his own crime performed on stage will surely be unmistakable:

Shakespeare wrote his plays primarily for performance, not for reading. The manuscripts of his plays were the property of his acting company; it was relatively unusual for plays to be printed for sale to the public. While Shakespeare took an active role in the publication of his longer poems, such as *Venus and Adonis*, he seems to have had virtually no interest in publishing his plays. The first complete collection, edited by two of his fellow-actors, was not produced until several years after his death.

Nevertheless, a number of Shakespeare's plays appeared as 'Quartos', slim booklets slightly larger than modern A5 in size, during his lifetime. Some of these Quartos were illicit 'pirated' versions of popular plays - attempts to reconstruct the originals from memory, from shorthand notes taken surreptitiously during a performance, or perhaps both. These unauthorised versions were generally of very poor quality.

In the case of *Hamlet*, a pirated Quarto was hurriedly produced in an early bid to cash in on the play's popularity. It was a particularly inept attempt, full of garbled and meaningless speeches, with events in the wrong order, speeches attributed to

Hamlet   I'll have these players
Play something like the murder of my father
Before mine uncle. I'll observe his looks;
I'll tent him to the quick.[1] If a do blench,[2]
I know my course.
                              . . . The play's the thing
Wherein I'll catch the conscience of the King.

[1] *open up and probe his wound*
[2] *if he flinches, if he reveals his pain*

---

the wrong characters, and numerous omissions and misunder-standings. What were to become the most famous words in the English language emerged, in the pirated version, as a hopeless jumble of half-remembered phrases:

To be, or not to be, ay there's the point,
To die, to sleep, is that all? Ay all:
No, to sleep, to dream, ay marry there it goes . . .

The text of the genuine *Hamlet*, authorised by Shakespeare's company, was published shortly afterwards in an attempt to undo the damage.

With most of the pirated Quartos, it is not known who supplied the publishers with their texts. However, in the case of *Hamlet* the culprit was almost certainly from within Shakespeare's own company - a short-term, hired actor, rather than a permanent member. Amidst the muddled, makeshift phrases of the pirated text, the few scenes in which the sentry Marcellus is on stage stand out by virtue of their accuracy, clarity and completeness.

> "What is it, then, that inhibits him in fulfilling the task set
> him by his father's ghost? The answer . . . lies in the particu-
> lar nature of the task. Hamlet is able to do anything - except
> take vengeance on the man who did away with his father and
> took that father's place with his mother, the man who shows
> him the repressed wishes of his own childhood realised. Thus the
> loathing which should drive him on to revenge is replaced in
> him by self-reproach, by scruples of conscience, which remind
> him that he is actually no better than the sinner whom he is to
> punish . . ."
>
> Sigmund Freud, *The Material and Sources of Dreams*, 1900

A meeting is staged

III, i

Rosencrantz and Guildenstern are reporting back to the King
on their conversation with Hamlet. They were unable to determine exactly what was going on in his mind, they tell Claudius:
he is obviously agitated in some way, but is being careful to
hide his real feelings behind his eccentric behaviour. However,
they report, the Prince was clearly delighted by the arrival of
the players.

Polonius confirms the young men's impression, adding that
Hamlet has specifically requested that the King should be in the
audience at tonight's performance. Claudius is pleased to hear of
Hamlet's enthusiasm, and asks Rosencrantz and Guildenstern to
encourage the Prince in his enjoyment of the players' compan-
ionship.

The King now asks to be left alone with Polonius and his
daughter; the time has come for the planned meeting between
Hamlet and Ophelia. Claudius explains his intention to

Gertrude. As she leaves, she suggests that Ophelia might indeed prove an ideal match for her son:

King	Her father and myself, lawful espials,[1]
	We'll so bestow ourselves that, seeing unseen,
	We may of their encounter frankly judge . . .
Queen	. . . for your part, Ophelia, I do wish
	That your good beauties be the happy cause
	Of Hamlet's wildness; so shall I hope your virtues
	Will bring him to his wonted way[2] again,
	To both your honours.
Ophelia	Madam, I wish it may.

[1] *legitimate spies*
[2] *restore him to his usual self*

Polonius gives Ophelia a prayer-book to read, so that she may appear to be deep in study when Hamlet arrives. He is sorry, he remarks, that they need to resort to such deception. His comment pierces the King's conscience, reminding him of a guilty secret of his own:

King	[*aside*] The harlot's cheek, beautied with
	plast'ring art,[1]
	Is not more ugly to the thing that helps it[2]
	Than is my deed to my most painted word.
	O heavy burden!

[1] *skill in applying cosmetics*
[2] *in comparison with its artificially beautified surface*

Hamlet is now approaching. Polonius and the King withdraw to observe the encounter in secrecy.

> "At Elsinore castle someone is hidden behind every curtain . . .
> Everything at Elsinore has been corroded by fear: marriage,
> love, friendship."
>
> Jan Kott, *Shakespeare our Contemporary*, 1965

Action and inaction: a meditation

Deep in thought, Hamlet does not notice Ophelia at first. A profound, urgent debate is going on in his mind. Should the pain
and the arbitrary misfortunes of life be endured stoically? Or
should the finality of death, bringing an end to all this suffering,
be welcomed, even chosen willingly?

Hamlet   To be, or not to be, that is the question:
              Whether 'tis nobler in the mind to suffer
              The slings and arrows of outrageous[1] fortune,
              Or to take arms against a sea of troubles[2]
              And by opposing end them.[3]

              [1] *indiscriminate, random*
              [2] *make a heroic but futile gesture against life's troubles*
              [3] *give up our lives in the unequal struggle, bringing
                  our troubles to an end*

Yet even death, he reflects, may not mean an end to suffering:

Hamlet   To die - to sleep,
                    No more; and by a sleep to say we end
                    The heart-ache and the thousand natural shocks
                    That flesh is heir to: 'tis a consummation
                    Devoutly to be wish'd. To die, to sleep;
                    To sleep, perchance to dream - ay, there's the rub:[1]
                    For in that sleep of death what dreams may come,
                    When we have shuffled off this mortal coil,[2]
                    Must give us pause . . .

        [1] *obstacle, snag*
        [2] *shaken off the hectic activity that entangles us in life*

If death were nothing more than a peaceful, dreamless sleep, suicide might seem the obvious way out of worldly torments. Fear of the unknown, though, compromises our resolve:

Hamlet   Who would fardels[1] bear,
                    To grunt and sweat under a weary life,
                    But that the dread of something after death,
                    The undiscover'd country, from whose bourn[2]
                    No traveller returns, puzzles the will,
                    And makes us rather bear those ills we have
                    Than fly to others that we know not of?

        [1] *burdens*
        [2] *boundary, border*

This fear of the unknown paralyses us in many situations. A decision not to act is often not a decision at all, then, but merely a surrender to our own anxieties:

Hamlet   Thus conscience[1] does make cowards of us all,
And thus the native hue of resolution
Is sicklied o'er with the pale cast of thought,[2]
And enterprises of great pitch and moment
With this regard their currents turn awry
And lose the name of action.[3]

[1] *consideration, contemplation*
[2] *the natural, healthy complexion of our courage is
quelled by the pallor of our deliberation*
[3] *in this way, plans for ambitious, important under-
takings fail to make headway, and end in inertia*

    Suddenly noticing Ophelia, Hamlet brings his deliberation to
an end. He sees that she is absorbed in her prayer-book: he asks
her to include him in her prayers.

Hamlet's behaviour continues to disturb

Ophelia greets Hamlet. He responds coolly. Ophelia reveals that
she has with her some gifts from the Prince, given when he was
courting her. Since his feelings seem to have changed, she now
wishes to return them:

Hamlet	I never gave you aught.[1]
Ophelia	My honour'd lord, you know right well you did,
	And with them words of so sweet breath
	compos'd
	As made the things more rich. Their perfume
	lost,
	Take these again;[2] for to the noble mind
	Rich gifts wax[3] poor when givers prove unkind.

[1] *anything*
[2] *back*
[3] *become*

Hamlet's mood seems to change suddenly; perhaps suspecting that Ophelia's gesture may be less than genuine, he becomes cynical and spiteful. He remarks, disparagingly, that it is difficult to find both beauty and virtue flourishing in one woman. If both qualities are present, virtue is bound to be the loser.

In Hamlet's eyes, his mother has already allowed her goodness to be corrupted, with her hasty marriage to Claudius: in the same way, Ophelia's beauty is likely to be her downfall. Warming to his theme, Hamlet launches into a stream of fierce invective against women, against men, against himself, against Polonius, against marriage. His disgust and pessimism come to a head as he orders Ophelia to the one place where she will be cut off from the temptations of courtship, desire and marriage:

Hamlet I have heard of your paintings[1] well enough. God hath given you one face and you make yourselves another. You jig and amble, and you lisp, you nickname God's creatures, and make your wantonness your ignorance.[2] Go to, I'll no more on't, it hath made me mad. I say we will have no mo[3] marriage. Those that are married already - all but one - shall live; the rest shall keep as they are. To a nunnery, go.

[1] *use of cosmetics*
[2] *behave provocatively whilst pretending to be innocent*
[3] *more*

Hamlet storms out. Ophelia is distraught; the only possible explanation for this outburst is that the Prince has lost his sanity. She is sorry both for him and for herself, now that his declarations of love have turned to wild raving:

Ophelia O, what a noble mind is here o'erthrown!
. . . Th'expectancy[1] and rose of the fair state,
The glass of fashion and the mould of form,[2]
Th'observ'd[3] of all observers, quite, quite down!
And I, of ladies most deject and wretched,
That suck'd the honey of his music vows,
Now see that noble and most sovereign reason
Like sweet bells jangled out of tune and harsh . . .

[1] *the anticipated successor to the throne*
[2] *regarded by all as a model of appearance and conduct*
[3] *admired, respected*

King Claudius and Polonius, who have witnessed both Hamlet's solitary debate and his furious attack on Ophelia, now emerge from their hiding-place. The King, unlike his adviser, sees no signs of love in the Prince's behaviour: nor does he think, with Ophelia, that Hamlet is simply deranged. He is sure that something sinister is lurking in the young man's mind:

King   Love? His affections do not that way tend,
      Nor what he spake, though it lack'd form a little,
      Was not like madness. There's something in his
       soul
      O'er which his melancholy sits on brood,
      And I do doubt[1] the hatch and the disclose[2]
      Will be some danger . . .

[1] *fear*
[2] *the emergence and revelation*

Claudius has already decided on the next move. He will shortly send Hamlet away to England, he tells Polonius, under the pretext of a diplomatic mission. The voyage, with its change of scenery and company, may help to lift Hamlet's oppressive mood of melancholy. Polonius agrees, but he still clings to the theory that the Prince is suffering from Ophelia's earlier rejection of his advances. He asks the King to sanction one final attempt to eavesdrop on the Prince before sending him away. Claudius gives his consent:

Polonius   . . . after the play
                    Let his queen-mother all alone entreat him
                    To show his grief, let her be round[1] with him,
                    And I'll be plac'd, so please you, in the ear
                    Of all their conference.[2] If she find him not,[3]
                    To England send him; or confine him where
                    Your wisdom best shall think.
King   It shall be so.
                    Madness in great ones must not unwatch'd go.

[1] *frank, plain-spoken*
[2] *within earshot of their conversation*
[3] *if she cannot establish the truth about him*

"*The world will corrupt Ophelia as it has corrupted Gertrude; Gertrude has become a whore, a fate that Hamlet wishes Ophelia to avoid, so he must therefore shock her, even by denying his feelings of love. This reading, however, still leaves Gertrude a whore, but it does also neatly reflect another comfortable misogynistic position that the play's commentators have often pandered to: not all women are whores; some are Madonnas. Certainly the play as seen through the male characters' perceptions seems to support this position.*"

Kay Stanton, *Hamlet's Whores*, in *New Essays on Hamlet*, 1994

A lecture on stagecraft for the players

III, ii

Preparations are under way at the court for the evening's entertainment. The players are to perform a tragedy, 'The Murder of Gonzago'. Hamlet, determined to provoke a reaction from the King, has supplied some extra material depicting the murder of his own father at Claudius's hands.

Hamlet is giving careful instructions to the players on the delivery of the additional lines that he has written. Soon, carried away by his passion for the stage, he is lecturing them at length on the art of acting, and warning them against some of the pitfalls:

Hamlet	Speak the speech, I pray you, as I pronounced it to you, trippingly on the tongue; but if you mouth it as many of your players do, I had as lief[1] the town-crier spoke my lines. Nor do not saw the air too much with your hand, thus, but use all gently . . . O, it offends me to the soul to hear a robustious periwig-pated fellow[2] tear a passion to tatters, to very rags, to split the ears of the groundlings . . .[3]

[1] *I'd just as soon*
[2] *blustering actor in a wig*
[3] *to thrill the spectators standing in the yard around the stage, who have bought the cheapest tickets*

Overacting must be avoided at all costs, explains the Prince as the players listen in tactful silence. Stage performances should be lifelike, with the aim of leading the audience to a better understanding of themselves and their world.

Hamlet finally expounds his pet hate, rounding on comic actors who will do anything to raise a laugh, even if it means ad-libbing, laughing at their own jokes, and interrupting the action of the play:

Hamlet   . . . let those that play your clowns speak no more
than is set down for them - for there be of them
that will themselves laugh, to set on some
quantity of barren[1] spectators to laugh too . . .
That's villainous, and shows a most pitiful
ambition in the fool that uses it.

[1] *mindless, uncritical*

The players leave to prepare for the performance. Polonius appears: Hamlet questions him, anxious to confirm that the King will be present at the play, then sends him off to ensure that the players' preparations are going smoothly.

Hamlet's views on clowning may well be a reflection of Shakespeare's own. The comic actor of Shakespeare's company, Will Kempe, left around the time that *Hamlet* was being written. His preference had always been for crude, slapstick humour, and he was notorious for his constant interruption and improvisation.

Kempe's successor, Robert Armin, had a witty, verbose style, more suited to the sophisticated comic roles that Shakespeare was now developing. The precise reasons for Kempe's departure are not known, but it is generally believed that Shakespeare and his colleagues were heartily glad to be rid of their irrepressible clown.

The audience assembles

Hamlet's old friend Horatio now joins him. As ever, Hamlet is glad of his company; the two of them have always been able to talk freely and sincerely, with no fear of ulterior motives or false praise. The Prince has always admired his friend's stoicism, his calm acceptance of life's unpredictability:

Hamlet   . . . thou hast been
    As one, in suff'ring all, that suffers nothing,[1]
    A man that Fortune's buffets and rewards
    Hast ta'en with equal thanks . . .
         Give me that man
    That is not passion's slave, and I will wear him
    In my heart's core, ay, in my heart of heart,
    As I do thee.

   [1] *one who endures everything equably, and thereby*
    avoids suffering

The Prince has a request to make to his trusted friend. He reveals that the play they are about to see will depict his father's murder. Every detail will be shown just as the ghost of the old King described. Hamlet intends to watch Claudius's reaction intently, and he asks Horatio to do the same. If the King betrays no sign of guilt, Hamlet will be forced to conclude that the ghost was an evil spirit sent to trouble him. Horatio promises to keep his eyes fixed on Claudius.

A trumpet sounds: Claudius and Gertrude are on their way. As Horatio hurries to find a suitable vantage-point, Hamlet tells him that he will again start playing the role of madman that he has been adopting in court.

The King and Queen now arrive, with a train of attendants and guards. Among their retinue are Polonius and his daughter, and Hamlet's friends Rosencrantz and Guildenstern. The King greets Hamlet, but can make nothing of his answer. However, behind the Prince's obscure comments lies a hint that he is starting to suspect Claudius's intentions towards him:

King	How fares[1] our cousin Hamlet?
Hamlet	Excellent, i'faith, of the chameleon's dish. I eat the air,[2] promise-crammed. You cannot feed capons[3] so.
King	I have nothing with this answer, Hamlet.

[1] *deliberately misinterpreted by Hamlet as referring to feeding*
[2] *an ancient belief held that chameleons lived on air*
[3] *a bird that was specially fattened for the table*

Hamlet turns to Polonius, and asks about his own acting experience. Polonius proudly recalls his moment of fame:

Polonius	I did enact Julius Caesar. I was killed i'th' Capitol. Brutus killed me.

I did enact Julius Caesar.

Shakespeare is almost certainly enjoying a theatrical in-joke. By far the best-known play about Caesar was his own *Julius Caesar*, first performed only a year or so before, and, like *Hamlet*, a great success with the public. In all probability, the actor now playing Polonius had indeed played Caesar: and the actor now playing Hamlet had taken the part of Brutus.

The players are about to enter, and the Queen asks her son to sit next to her. Hamlet refuses, and instead approaches Ophelia, an action that Polonius eagerly draws to the King's attention.

In contrast to his earlier outburst, Hamlet now adopts a different attitude towards Ophelia. He becomes playful and teasing, even obscene; but the revulsion arising from his mother's remarriage is never far from his thoughts:

Hamlet	What should a man do but be merry? For look you how cheerfully my mother looks and my father died within's two hours.
Ophelia	Nay, 'tis twice two months, my lord.
Hamlet	So long? Nay then, let the devil wear black . . Then there's hope a great man's memory may outlive his life half a year.

A murder is enacted

The players come on stage. As a prelude to the play, they perform a dumb-show in which the plot is acted out in silence. Hamlet has briefed the actors carefully, and has ensured that the play will reflect the truth of his father's death as recounted by the ghost.

The dumb-show commences. The Player King and Queen are seen embracing affectionately in a garden: the King then lies down to sleep on a bank of flowers, and she leaves him. Another man steals in, pours poison into the sleeping King's ear, and runs off. The Queen returns to find her husband dead, and gives a passionate display of grief. The body is carried off.

The poisoner returns to the stage, and offers the Queen gifts in an attempt to win her love: she refuses his attentions at first, but in the end accepts his love gladly.

Following the dumb-show, the stage is cleared, and the play begins. The Player King and Queen make their entrance again, and address one another lovingly. They have been married for thirty years, declares the King. The Queen immediately expresses the hope that their happiness will continue for another thirty years: however, she is concerned that he has been in poor health of late.

The King admits that she is right, and gently suggests that, if he should die, the Queen will have to think about remarrying. She is aghast at the idea. Such an action would be a betrayal of their love, and would drag her down to the level of a murderer:

Player King	. . . thou shalt live in this fair world behind,
	Honour'd, belov'd; and haply one as kind
	For husband shalt thou -
Player Queen	O confound the rest.
	Such love must needs be treason in my breast.
	In second husband let me be accurst;
	None wed the second but who kill'd the first.

Despite his wife's passionate denial, the King remains sure that she will remarry. Any resolution made in the heat of a strong emotion, he reflects, is bound to lose its impetus once that emotion has cooled:

Player King	What to ourselves in passion we propose,
	The passion ending, doth the purpose lose.
	The violence of either grief or joy
	Their own enactures with themselves destroy.

Besides, continues the King, love and friendship are not permanent or absolute; they are likely to change as our fortunes change. The world is an unpredictable place, and our plans, our resolutions and our promises are all likely to come to grief in the fullness of time.

The Queen remains determined. She declares zealously that she will never marry again if she should become a widow. The

King does not pursue the argument. He is weary, he says, and asks his wife to leave him to sleep on a grassy bank.

As the Player Queen makes her exit, Hamlet turns to his mother. She, of course, has done precisely what the Player Queen has sworn never to do, and both she and Claudius are uneasy about the content of the play. Hamlet assures them ironically that it is only make-believe. Even the crime that is about to be staged is just play-acting:

Hamlet	Madam, how like you this play?
Queen	The lady doth protest too much,[1] methinks.
Hamlet	O, but she'll keep her word.
King	Have you heard the argument?[2] Is there no offence in't?
Hamlet	No, no, they do but jest - poison in jest. No offence[3] i'th' world.

[1] *overstates her feelings, is too bombastic*
[2] *plot, content*
[3] *crime*

"Here on the stage before us is a play of false appearances in which an actor called the player-king is playing. But there is also on the stage Claudius, another player-king, who is a spectator of this player. And there is on the stage, besides, a prince who is a spectator of both these player-kings and who plays with great intensity a player's role himself. And around these kings and that prince is a group of courtly spectators . . . And lastly there are ourselves, an audience watching all these audiences who are also players. Where, it may suddenly occur to us to ask, does the playing end?"

Maynard Mack, *The World of Hamlet*, 1953

Hamlet goes on to explain that the play - which in his own secretly adapted version he christens 'The Mousetrap' - is based on a real murder carried out in Vienna. Although the actions presented in it are evil, says Hamlet wryly, the play can do no harm to innocent people such as himself and Claudius.

A new character now appears on stage and approaches the sleeping Player King. Hamlet continues with his explanation, breaking off to aim a few bawdy comments at Ophelia:

Hamlet	This is one Lucianus, nephew to the King.
Ophelia	You are as good as a chorus,[1] my lord.
Hamlet	I could interpret between you and your love if I could see the puppets dallying.[2]
Ophelia	You are keen, my lord, you are keen.
Hamlet	It would cost you a groaning to take off my edge.[3]
Ophelia	Still better, and worse.

[1] *an actor who describes and interprets the play's action*

[2] *if I were watching you and your lover embracing, I could provide a commentary*

[3] *to blunt the keen edge of my desire; to satisfy my lust*

This is one Lucianus, nephew to the King.

If Hamlet's 'Mousetrap' were a recreation of the murder of his father, we should expect the murderer to be described as the King's brother, not his nephew.

Hamlet's words mean that the acting out of the murder is combined with a hint of his own intended revenge. As nephew to King Claudius himself, he appears to make both a private accusation and a public threat.

Lucianus announces his presence. He is carrying a phial of poison distilled from deadly plants. This is the perfect opportunity to carry out his crime, he declares: the King is asleep, and no-one else is present. Without further ado he pours his poison into the King's ear.

Hamlet continues with his commentary, hoping all the time for a response from Claudius as he sees his secret crime revealed on the stage.

Finally, to Hamlet's delight, his stratagem proves successful. The King, unable to watch the scene being played out in front of him, rushes out, followed by his courtiers. He cries out for light, and Polonius orders the torchbearers to accompany him. The performance breaks up in confusion:

Ophelia	The King rises.
Hamlet	What, frighted with false fire?[1]
Queen	How fares my lord?
Polonius	Give o'er the play.
King	Give me some light. Away.
Polonius	Lights, lights, lights.

[1] *frightened by the firing of blanks*

Hamlet is resolved

Hamlet and Horatio remain behind as the audience and players disperse. Hamlet is jubilant at the success of his scheme. He confers excitedly with his friend, who confirms that the King did indeed react violently at the mention of poison.

The ghost's account of King Hamlet's death has been proved true. In his excitement, Hamlet calls for the actors to return and play some music for him.

Rosencrantz and Guildenstern come to join Hamlet. The episode they have just witnessed has left them confused and worried, and they are at a loss to understand Hamlet's light-hearted remarks. The King is in a state of furious agitation, they report: and the Queen, also deeply shaken by the performance that Hamlet has just staged, wants to talk to him in private.

Hamlet's two friends are still anxious to establish the cause of the strange moods that seem to have afflicted him recently. He does not reveal anything of his father's murder to the two men. Instead, he tells them that he is troubled by his impatience to succeed to the throne:

Rosencrantz   Good my lord, what is your cause of distemper? You do surely bar the door upon your own liberty[1] if you deny your griefs to your friend.
Hamlet   Sir, I lack advancement.
Rosencrantz   How can that be, when you have the voice of the King himself for your succession in Denmark?
Hamlet   Ay, sir, but while the grass grows[2] - the proverb is something[3] musty.

> [1] *you keep yourself locked in the prison of your own unhappiness*
> [2] *'While the grass grows, the horse starves': there is a limit to how long I can wait*
> [3] *somewhat*

The players come back, ready to provide the music that Hamlet had called for. However, the Prince's mood has changed; his friends' efforts to investigate his behaviour are starting to anger him. Hamlet takes a recorder from one of the actors and asks Guildenstern to play it. He replies that he cannot. Hamlet asks again, and again: Guildenstern can only repeat, in embarrassment, that he has no idea what to do. All the more reason, argues Hamlet, to leave him alone:

Hamlet	I do beseech you.
Guildenstern	I know no touch of it, my lord.
Hamlet	It is as easy as lying. Govern these ventages[1] with your fingers and thumb, give it breath with your mouth, and it will discourse most eloquent music. Look you, these are the stops.
Guildenstern	But these cannot I command to any utterance of harmony. I have not the skill.
Hamlet	Why, look you now, how unworthy a thing you make of me. You would play upon me, you would seem to know my stops, you would pluck out the heart of my mystery . . . 'Sblood, do you think I am easier to be played on than a pipe?

[1] *finger holes*

Polonius now arrives. He has been sent by the Queen, and urges Hamlet to join his mother at once. Hamlet refuses to be hurried, and asks the others to leave him.

Alone, Hamlet's longing for revenge starts to well up again. Although it is the King who must be punished, Hamlet knows that in his rage he could even put his mother to death. He swears to himself that he will spare her, just as the spirit of his father had commanded:

Hamlet   'Tis now the very witching time of night,
            When churchyards yawn[1] and hell itself
                breathes out
            Contagion to this world. Now could I drink hot
                blood,
            And do such bitter business as the day
            Would quake to look on. Soft, now to my
                mother . . .
            Let me be cruel, not unnatural.
            I will speak daggers to her, but use none.

        [1] *open their graves*

"The new resolution that comes to Hamlet when the Ghost's story is confirmed reveals not so much an acceptance of duty as an exultation in hate, vindictiveness, blood lust. In this mood the hero comes closest to the villain he would damn . . ."

Harold Jenkins, Arden edition of *Hamlet*, 1982

An opportunity for revenge

III, iii

Claudius's plan to remove Hamlet from Elsinore for a while, by sending him on a diplomatic mission to England, has taken on a new urgency. It is now startlingly clear to Claudius that his nephew knows about the murder of King Hamlet and is ready to seek vengeance.

Claudius has summoned Rosencrantz and Guildenstern to his presence. Hamlet's madness now poses a real threat to the King's life, he tells them. He is shortly sending Hamlet abroad, and they are to accompany him.

The two men accept their duty willingly. Any threat to the King puts the entire state of Denmark in danger:

Rosencrantz   The cess[1] of majesty
Dies not alone, but like a gulf[2] doth draw
What's near it with it. Or it is a massy wheel
Fix'd on the summit of the highest mount,
To whose huge spokes ten thousand lesser things
Are mortis'd and adjoin'd, which when it falls,
Each small annexment, petty consequence,
Attends the boist'rous ruin.[3]

[1] *ceasing, death*
[2] *whirlpool*
[3] *shares in the tumultuous destruction*

Rosencrantz and Guildenstern hurry off to prepare for the journey. As they leave, Polonius arrives. He reports that Hamlet is on his way to see the Queen, and tells Claudius that he intends to hide in the Queen's room and eavesdrop on their conversation. He sets off at once, leaving Claudius on his own.

Overcome with misery, the King now contemplates his guilt. He has tried to pray for mercy, but his awareness of his dreadful crime makes it impossible:

King   O, my offence is rank, it smells to heaven;
It hath the primal eldest curse[1] upon't -
A brother's murder. Pray can I not,
Though inclination be as sharp as will,
My stronger guilt defeats my strong intent,
And, like a man to double business bound,[2]
I stand in pause where I shall first begin,
And both neglect.

> [1] *God's curse on Cain, who murdered his brother Abel*
> [2] *with two duties to carry out*

He cannot pray for forgiveness, he realises, because he is still enjoying the fruits of his crime; and heavenly justice, unlike justice on earth, cannot be evaded with bribery or trickery. Nevertheless, he tries once more, wretchedly, to pray.

It is at this moment that Hamlet enters. The King is alone, kneeling, and defenceless; Hamlet is presented with the perfect opportunity for revenge. He draws his sword:

Hamlet   Now might I do it pat, now a[1] is a-praying.
And now I'll do't. And so a goes to heaven;
And so am I reveng'd.

> [1] *he*

Hamlet pauses. If he kills Claudius now, in prayer, his soul will go to heaven: surely, he reasons, this is not a fit end for the man who murdered his father? After all, Claudius did not show such consideration when he poisoned King Hamlet in his sleep. Instead, Hamlet decides to take his revenge at a time when he can be sure of sending Claudius to damnation:

Hamlet   Up, sword, and know thou a more horrid hent:[1]
When he is drunk asleep, or in his rage,
Or in th'incestuous pleasure of his bed,
At game a-swearing, or about some act
That has no relish of salvation in't,
Then trip him, that his heels may kick at heaven
And that his soul may be as damn'd and black
As hell, whereto it goes.

[1] *you will be used on a more terrible occasion*

Replacing his sword in its sheath, Hamlet leaves the King at prayer and sets off to see Gertrude.

Claudius, unaware of Hamlet's brief presence in the room, now gives up his futile attempt at praying. He realises, with despair, that there is repentance in the words of his prayers, but not in his soul:

King   My words fly up, my thoughts remain below.
Words without thoughts never to heaven go.

"There is . . . a sense of improvisation that we get in Hamlet; *that the dramatist is sometimes wondering, like his hero, what he is going to do next."*

Robert Speaight, *Shakespeare: The Man and his Achievement,* 1977

A deadly error

III, iv

Polonius has arrived in Queen Gertrude's room, intending to listen to her conversation with Hamlet. He encourages her to be firm with her son, and to emphasise how much tolerance has been shown to his outrageous behaviour. Hearing Hamlet approach, he hides behind the tapestry hanging on the wall.

Hamlet now enters. An angry exchange between mother and son immediately erupts:

Queen	Hamlet, thou hast thy father[1] much offended.
Hamlet	Mother, you have my father[2] much offended.
Queen	Come, come, you answer with an idle tongue.
Hamlet	Go, go, you question with a wicked tongue.

> [1] *Claudius*
> [2] *King Hamlet*

Unable to make sense of his answers, the Queen gets up to leave. Hamlet forces her to sit down again, determined to confront her with her own disloyalty to the murdered King. Unsure of her son's intentions, and fearing that he may even try to kill her, Gertrude calls out for help. Polonius, from his hiding-place, does the same; Hamlet, hearing a voice, impulsively draws his sword and thrusts it into the tapestry. The cry of a dying man is heard.

The Queen is horrified. Hamlet, however, remains unmoved. It is her marriage to the murderous Claudius - an act, in Hamlet's mind, as wicked as the murder itself - that he wishes to force to her attention. He gives a brief, dismissive farewell to the dead Polonius:

Queen	O me, what hast thou done?
Hamlet	Nay, I know not.
	Is it the King? [*Lifts up the arras¹ and discovers*
	Polonius, dead.]
Queen	O what a rash and bloody deed is this!
Hamlet	A bloody deed. Almost as bad, good mother,
	As kill a king and marry with his brother.
Queen	As kill a king?
Hamlet	Ay, lady, it was my word. -
	Thou wretched, rash, intruding fool, farewell.
	I took thee for thy better. Take thy fortune:
	Thou find'st to be too busy² is some danger.

¹ *tapestry wall-hanging*
² *inquisitive, scheming*

Hamlet continues with his passionate denunciation of the Queen. He brings out two pictures, one of the dead King and one of Claudius. In the first he sees all the qualities of true manhood: grace, beauty, courage, honour. In the second, he sees only corruption and rottenness:

Hamlet	Look you now what follows.
	Here is your husband, like a mildew'd ear
	Blasting¹ his wholesome brother. Have you eyes?

¹ *blighting, infecting, like a diseased ear of corn*

Gertrude's marriage to the brutish Claudius, so soon after the King's death, continues to horrify and bewilder Hamlet. Perhaps their sexual relationship began while King Hamlet was still alive, he suggests: perhaps she was even aware of the murder. He cannot contain his feelings of revulsion as he envisages her in Claudius's embrace:

Hamlet	Nay, but to live
	In the rank sweat of an enseamed[1] bed,
	Stew'd in corruption, honeying and making love
	Over the nasty sty!
Queen	O speak to me no more.
	These words like daggers enter in my ears.
	No more, sweet Hamlet.
Hamlet	A murderer and a villain,
	A slave that is not twentieth part the tithe[2]
	Of your precedent lord, a vice of kings,
	A cutpurse[3] of the empire and the rule . . .

[1] *greasy, filthy*
[2] *tenth*
[3] *thief*

Hamlet's angry stream of accusations is suddenly interrupted as the ghost of the old King appears in the room. He is no longer in his warlike armour, but in his everyday clothes. He has come, he says, to renew Hamlet's determination to carry out the task of revenge which remains, as yet, undone. He asks Hamlet to comfort his mother rather than trouble her with further censure.

This time, the ghost is visible only to Hamlet. Gertrude, seeing her son staring wildly into empty space, takes this as yet another sign of his madness. Hamlet, amazed that she cannot see or hear anything, tries to persuade her of the ghost's presence: but it remains invisible to the Queen, and eventually drifts out of the room.

Hamlet warns the Queen against corruption

Calmer and more gentle now, Hamlet implores Gertrude to face up to the truth of Claudius's wickedness and her own complicity. It is only through repentance, and renunciation of Claudius's love, that she will cleanse herself of the evil that now taints her. He urges her to reject the tenderness she feels for her husband:

Hamlet   Mother, for love of grace,
                        Lay not that flattering unction to your soul,
                        That not your trespass but my madness speaks.[1]
                        It will but skin and film[2] the ulcerous place,
                        Whiles rank corruption, mining[3] all within,
                        Infects unseen . . .
Queen   O Hamlet, thou hast cleft my heart in twain.
Hamlet   O throw away the worser part of it
                        And live the purer with the other half.

[1] *do not try to console yourself with the idea that the problem is my madness rather than your wrongdoing*
[2] *it will only cover, allow skin to grow over*
[3] *eating away, undermining*

It will but skin and film the ulcerous place . . .

In *Hamlet*, more than in any other play, Shakespeare makes frequent mention of sickness and medicine. Over twenty such images - of diseases of the skin, abscesses, hidden tumours, painful symptoms and desperate remedies - reinforce the atmosphere of corruption and secrecy that envelops Elsinore.

The force of habit allows evil to thrive, believes Hamlet, as people can easily ignore the sinful aspects of their everyday actions: in the same way, goodness can be made to flourish simply by the habitual carrying out of virtuous actions. He asks

Gertrude to resist the temptation to sleep with her husband tonight: gradually, abstinence will become a habit, and she will eventually free herself from his corrupting influence.

Turning to Polonius's lifeless body, Hamlet reflects that he seems to have been given the role both of punisher and of punished. He has inadvertently punished the old man for his meddling; at the same time, his own rashness has been punished by this death now on his hands, a death whose consequences are as yet unknown.

However, Gertrude remains Hamlet's main concern, and he reassures her that his harsh words spring from his compassion for her:

Hamlet   For this same lord
              I do repent; but heaven hath pleas'd it so,
              To punish me with this and this with me,
              That I must be their scourge and minister.[1]
              I will bestow[2] him, and will answer well
              The death I gave him. So, again, good night.
              I must be cruel only to be kind.

              [1] *agent of heaven's will*
              [2] *dispose of*

Before leaving, Hamlet urges his mother not to let Claudius seduce her into revealing the conversation that has taken place between them. He reminds her that he must go to England, with Rosencrantz and Guildenstern as his companions. He does not trust them in the slightest, and does not know what subterfuge has been planned, but relishes the prospect of outwitting the two of them:

Hamlet . . . 'tis the sport to have the enginer[1]
Hoist with his own petard,[2] and't shall go hard[3]
But I will delve one yard below their mines
And blow them at the moon.

[1] *builder of explosive devices*
[2] *blown into the air by his own bomb*
[3] *I'll be surprised if it turns out otherwise*

Hamlet says a final goodnight to his mother, and leaves, lugging the body of Polonius unceremoniously behind him.

. . . I must be their scourge and minister.

The word 'scourge' carried powerful overtones, suggesting someone chosen by God to deliver just retribution. The person selected, however, was not necessarily free from guilt himself, nor would his punishment of the guilty lead to his own salvation. The belief is succinctly expressed in another tragedy of the time, by two of Shakespeare's younger contemporaries:

. . . on lustfull Kings
Unlookt for suddaine deaths from God are sent,
But curst is he that is their instrument.

Beaumont and Fletcher, *The Maid's Tragedy*, 1610

Claudius is shaken

IV, i

The King comes into Gertrude's room to find out what Hamlet has said to her. He is horrified to learn about the impetuous killing of Polonius, and realises that he is likely to be held accountable:

King   O heavy deed!
    It had been so with us[1] had we been there.
    His liberty is full of threats to all -
    To you yourself, to us, to everyone.
    Alas, how shall this bloody deed be answer'd?[2]
    It will be laid to us, whose providence
    Should have kept short, restrain'd, and out of
        haunt[3]
    This mad young man.

[1] *this would have happened to me*
[2] *accounted for, explained*
[3] *kept on a short tether, away from company*

It was love for Hamlet, claims the King, that prevented them from taking action earlier. However, no further delay can be tolerated: Hamlet is to be sent away to England at first light tomorrow morning. He must be found at once.

Gertrude explains that Hamlet has gone to dispose of the body, and assures her husband that, despite his madness, there is still an essential goodness in her son that makes him truly remorseful for what he has done.

Claudius calls for Rosencrantz and Guildenstern. He instructs them to find Hamlet, and to carry Polonius's body into the chapel.

Hamlet's fate is sealed

IV, ii - iii

Rosencrantz and Guildenstern, along with the guards they have summoned, eventually manage to track Hamlet down. Remaining calm and respectful, as instructed by the King, they press Hamlet to tell them where the body is. His answers, full of veiled scorn for the King and the two men he is using as his agents, leave the others baffled. Hamlet gives nothing away about the whereabouts of the body, but readily agrees to go along with them to see the King.

Meanwhile, Claudius is in urgent conference with his advisers. He must be careful in his treatment of Hamlet, he realises; the Prince's popularity is widespread, and the people of Denmark will take his side. Nevertheless, drastic action may be necessary:

King   How dangerous is it that this man goes loose!
      Yet must not we put the strong law on him:
      He's lov'd of the distracted[1] multitude,
      Who like not in their judgment but their eyes,
      And where 'tis so, th'offender's scourge is
        weigh'd,[2]
      But never the offence.
          . . . Diseases desperate grown
      By desperate appliance[3] are reliev'd,
      Or not at all.

[1] *irrational, unthinking*
[2] *the punishment of the offender is considered*
[3] *treatment*

Hamlet's dispatch to England will go ahead, but will be presented as a journey that has been planned for some time, not a sudden reaction to his crime.

Rosencrantz and Guildenstern now return, bringing Hamlet with them. The King at once tries to establish where Polonius's body is, but, like his courtiers, is baffled by Hamlet's replies:

King	Now, Hamlet, where's Polonius?
Hamlet	At supper.
King	At supper? Where?
Hamlet	Not where he eats, but where a[1] is eaten. A certain convocation of politic worms[2] are e'en[3] at him.

[1] *he*

[2] *an assembly of scheming worms*

[3] *at this moment*

Finally, Hamlet reveals where he has put the body, and the King sends some attendants off at once to find it. Hamlet reassures them that there is no need to hurry; Polonius will wait for them.

The King now breaks the news to Hamlet: for his own safety, he is to be sent to England immediately. Hamlet shows no surprise. He says a brief, sardonic farewell, and sets off to prepare for the voyage. Claudius orders his attendants to follow him closely and make sure that he is on board ship, ready to depart, as soon as possible.

When the others have left, Claudius reveals the fate that awaits Hamlet on his mission to England. The letter that is to be delivered to the English King contains an explicit command, one which must be carried out immediately. England has recently suffered a terrible, bloody defeat at the hands of the Danes, and the English King is sure to obey:

King	And England, if my love thou hold'st at aught . . .
	. . . thou mayst not coldly set[1]
	Our sovereign process, which imports at full,
	By letters congruing to that effect,
	The present[2] death of Hamlet. Do it, England;
	For like the hectic[3] in my blood he rages,
	And thou must cure me.

[1] *you cannot disregard*
[2] *immediate*
[3] *fever*

All that remains for Claudius is the torment of waiting for the news that his order has been carried out. He is convinced that he will never achieve happiness and security as long as Hamlet is alive.

> "I had always felt an aversion from Hamlet: a creeping, unclean thing he seems . . . His nasty poking and sniffing at his mother, his setting traps for the King, his conceited perversion with Ophelia make him always intolerable. The character is repulsive in its conception, based on self-dislike and a spirit of disintegration. There is, I think, this strain of cold dislike, or self-dislike, through much of the Renaissance art, and through all the later Shakespeare . . ."
>
> D. H. Lawrence, *Twilight in Italy*, 1913

Fortinbras leads his army to battle

IV, iv

Fortinbras, the Prince of Norway, has arrived in Denmark at the head of a great army. His earlier threat to attack Denmark, and recover the lands won from his father by King Hamlet, was averted by Claudius. Instead, Fortinbras aims to conquer a stretch of territory in Poland. An agreement has been reached between Norway and Denmark that his troops can pass safely over Danish soil on their way to the battle.

A captain is dispatched to inform Claudius of the arrival of Fortinbras and his army, and to confirm their safe conduct through Denmark. As the army marches on, Hamlet arrives, about to embark on his sea-voyage to England. He questions the captain, and is amazed at the scale of the military operation for such a small prize:

"There is never an ideal production of Hamlet; *any interpretation must limit. For our decade I think the play will be about the disillusionment which produces an apathy of the will so deep that commitment to politics, to religion or to life is impossible . . . Hamlet is always on the brink of action, but something inside him, this disease of disillusionment, stops the final, committed action. It is an emotion which you can encounter in the young today . . ."*

Peter Hall, discussing his 1965 production of *Hamlet* at the Royal Shakespeare Theatre

---

Captain	Truly to speak, and with no addition,[1]
	We go to gain a little patch of ground
	That hath in it no profit but the name.
	To pay five ducats - five - I would not farm it . . .[2]
Hamlet	Why, then the Polack never will defend it.
Captain	Yes, it is already garrison'd.

[1] *exaggeration*
[2] *buy the lease*

The captain sets off to see the King. Hamlet, alone, re-proaches himself for his failure to act quickly to avenge his fa-ther's murder. He is painfully aware that this show of decisive military might is in sharp contrast to his own delay. Perhaps he has failed to think clearly about what is required of him; or per-haps he has thought too much:

Hamlet	How all occasions do inform against me,
	And spur my dull revenge.
	. . . whether it be
	Bestial oblivion, or some craven scruple
	Of thinking too precisely on th'event[1] -
	A thought which, quarter'd, hath but one part wisdom
	And ever three parts coward - I do not know
	Why yet I live to say this thing's to do,
	Sith[2] I have cause, and will, and strength, and means
	To do't.

[1] *consequences*
[2] *since*

The waste and futility of the planned invasion make him all the more determined to be ruthless in pursuing his own objective:

Hamlet   How stand I then . . .

           . . . while to my shame I see
The imminent death of twenty thousand men
That, for a fantasy and trick of fame,[1]
Go to their graves like beds, fight for a plot
Whereon the numbers cannot try the cause,
Which is not tomb enough and continent
To hide the slain?[2] O, from this time forth
My thoughts be bloody or be nothing worth.

[1] *for the illusion of honour, and the trivial prize
   of fame*
[2] *a plot which is too small to hold those who are
   fighting over it, or even to bury all the dead*

Another casualty

IV, v

An attendant informs the Queen that Ophelia, daughter of the murdered Polonius, wishes to speak to her. He warns her that the young woman is behaving very strangely, and her speech is disjointed and almost incomprehensible. The Queen agrees, unwillingly, to see her. She is so racked with guilt and worry herself that she fears the slightest upset will devastate her:

Queen   [*aside*] To my sick soul, as sin's true nature is,
               Each toy[1] seems prologue to some great amiss.
               So full of artless jealousy[2] is guilt,
               It spills[3] itself in fearing to be spilt.

    [1] *trifle, minor mishap*
    [2] *indiscriminate suspicion*
    [3] *destroys*

Ophelia enters. It is clear at once that she has succumbed to madness. She speaks little, singing instead snatches of old ballads. In the first, a young maid laments the disappearance of her lover, only to learn that he has died:

Ophelia   [*sings*] *He is dead and gone, lady,*
                 He is dead and gone,
           At his head a grass-green turf,
             At his heels a stone.

She changes the conventional ending of the song. This lover went to his grave without the tears befitting the death of a loved one:

Ophelia   [*sings*] *White his shroud as the mountain snow*
                      Larded[1] with sweet flowers
                    Which bewept to the grave did not go
                      With true-love showers.[2]

[1] *bedecked*
[2] *tears*

Although she urges the Queen to listen to her song, Ophelia gives no clue as to its meaning. The King, who now joins his wife, immediately concludes that Ophelia is grieving distractedly for her dead father: however, in her song there is more than a hint of mourning for the death of Hamlet's love.

Claudius tries, unsuccessfully, to communicate with Ophelia. She responds with another song, this time the story of a maid seduced and then deserted; the same plight that both her father and her brother had warned her against so strongly when she and Hamlet were sweethearts.

Still patient and gentle in her madness, Ophelia takes her leave. The King orders his attendants to follow her and tend her with care.

Claudius and Gertrude are now alone. The King muses despairingly on the series of disasters that has afflicted Elsinore. The latest and most serious threat is the return of Polonius's son Laertes, who will undoubtedly demand vengeance for his father's death:

King   O Gertrude, Gertrude,
When sorrows come, they come not single spies,[1]
But in battalions. First, her father slain;
Next, your son gone, and he most violent author
Of his own just remove; the people muddied,
Thick and unwholesome[2] in their thoughts and
    whispers
For good Polonius' death - and we have done but
    greenly
In hugger-mugger to inter him;[3] poor Ophelia
Divided from herself and her fair judgment,
Without the which we are pictures, or mere
    beasts;
Last, and as much containing as all these,
Her brother is in secret come from France . . .

[1] *as solitary soldiers in the vanguard*
[2] *the people confused and suspicious*
[3] *we have been hasty and foolish in burying him so
secretively*

---

*"The hero of one plot, Hamlet is in effect the villain of the other,
casting an inescapable doubt upon his heroic role."*

Charles Boyce, *Shakespeare A to Z*, 1990

Laertes demands revenge

As Claudius is reflecting on the rumours linking him to the
death of Polonius, a violent disturbance is heard outside the castle. A messenger rushes in to tell the King that a riotous mob,
headed by Laertes, is flooding into the castle, overpowering his

guards. Heedless of law and tradition, the mob is demanding the instatement of Laertes as King of Denmark.

No sooner has the messenger given his warning than the doors of Claudius's room burst open and Laertes storms in, demanding to speak to the King. Ordering his eager followers to remain outside, he confronts Claudius at once. Barely able to contain his rage, he demands to know the truth about his father.

Gertrude holds Laertes back, fearing for her husband's safety: but Claudius tells her, calmly, to let him go, and asks the young man to express his grievance. Laertes announces that all he wants is revenge for his father's murder. Considerations of morality, loyalty to the King, or earthly or divine judgement, are of no importance to him:

Laertes	To hell, allegiance! Vows to the blackest devil!
	Conscience and grace, to the profoundest pit!
	I dare damnation. To this point I stand,
	That both the worlds I give to negligence,[1]
	Let come what comes, only I'll be reveng'd
	Most thoroughly for my father.

> [1] *I hold the concerns of this world, and the next,*
> *in contempt*

Remaining calm, Claudius assures Laertes that he is innocent of any involvement in his father's death: he knows the culprit, though, and can reveal his identity.

A girl's voice is suddenly heard outside the room. Laertes' sister Ophelia wanders in, distracted, singing snatches of songs as before, and carrying a handful of wild flowers. She gives no sign of recognition to her brother. Laertes is devastated:

Laertes   O rose of May!
Dear maid - kind sister - sweet Ophelia -
O heavens, is't possible a young maid's wits
Should be as mortal as an old man's life?

Laertes vows that this madness, like the death of Polonius which he believes to have been its cause, must also be revenged. Ophelia's gentleness makes him all the more determined. He watches in anguish as she hands out her flowers:

Ophelia   There's rosemary, that's for remembrance - pray
you, love, remember. And there is pansies, that's
for thoughts.

With unconscious irony, Ophelia hands some columbine, a flower symbolising unfaithfulness in marriage, to the Queen: while the King receives a sprig of rue, the herb of repentance. She sings a final ballad about the death of a loved one, and takes her leave.

The King assures Laertes that he shares in his grief, and urges him to investigate his father's death with the help of whichever friends he chooses. If Laertes finds evidence of Claudius's involvement, however indirect, he will be free to take the King's life, property and crown: if not, Claudius proposes, the two of them should work together to punish the guilty party.

An unexpected message

IV, vi

Some seafarers come to Elsinore asking to speak in private to Horatio, Hamlet's old friend. They have a letter from the Prince, who was recently sent off, along with Rosencrantz and Guildenstern, on his fateful voyage to England.

Claudius's plan for Hamlet has miscarried. The letter reveals that Hamlet did not reach England: his ship was attacked by pirates, and after a struggle he was held prisoner on board the pirate ship. Eventually, the pirates set Hamlet down in Denmark, and he is now in hiding. The men delivering the letter, writes Hamlet, will be able to lead Horatio to his hiding-place. In the meantime, Hamlet's ship has continued on its way to England with Rosencrantz and Guildenstern still on board. He has some momentous news, he implies, both about his voyage and about his two companions.

Hamlet asks Horatio to ensure that the sailors delivering the note are given access to the King, to whom he has written further letters. Once that is done, Horatio is to join the Prince as speedily as possible.

Claudius enlists the help of Laertes

IV, vii

The King has satisfied Laertes that he played no part in the death of Polonius. He has also explained that the true culprit, Hamlet, has even plotted to murder the King himself.

Laertes' rage has subsided, but his desire for revenge is as keen as before. He asks the King why Hamlet has not been punished for his crime. There were two considerations, alleges Claudius. First, the Queen is devoted to her son: Claudius in turn is devoted to her, and cannot help but be swayed by her compassion for the Prince. Secondly there is the question of the public reaction to Hamlet's punishment, which would undoubtedly be hostile: Hamlet is held in great affection by the people of Denmark, who always seem ready to forgive his faults. All this, however, does not mean that Hamlet will escape retribution. In fact, suggests Claudius, Laertes will soon hear some encouraging news.

Just as the King is reassuring Laertes that justice will be done, he is stunned by the arrival of an unexpected letter. It is from the very man whom he had sent to his death:

> *High and mighty, you shall know I am set naked[1] on*
> *your kingdom. Tomorrow shall I beg leave to see*
> *your kingly eyes, when I shall, first asking your*
> *pardon, thereunto recount the occasion of my*
> *sudden and more strange return.*
>   *Hamlet.*

[1] *stripped of all possessions*

The King is baffled. For a moment he suspects that the letter is a forgery; but the handwriting is undoubtedly Hamlet's. How he has managed to return, and what has happened to his two escorts, remain a mystery. Laertes, unaware of the King's plot, is glad of the news. He can now meet his enemy face to face:

Laertes   . . . let him come.
It warms the very sickness in my heart
That I shall live and tell him to his teeth,
'Thus diest thou'.

Thinking quickly, Claudius asks Laertes whether he will accept his guidance. As long as the King does not expect him to forgo his revenge, replies the young man, he will. The King explains that he has in mind a scheme which will result in Hamlet's certain death. It will be carried out in such a way that his death will seem accidental, even to his mother; better still, Laertes himself will have the satisfaction of administering the fatal stroke.

Claudius elaborates on his proposed scheme. Laertes' skill at fencing is well-known, he says; in fact, reports of his ability have made Hamlet jealous recently, and the Prince would dearly love to challenge him to a fencing-match. Interrupting his explanation, Claudius asks Laertes whether his resolve may be weakening. The response is unequivocal:

King   That we would do,[1]
We should do when we would: for this 'would'
       changes
And hath abatements[2] and delays as many
As there are tongues, are hands, are accidents . . .
       . . . But to the quick of th'ulcer:[3]
Hamlet comes back; what would you undertake
To show yourself in deed your father's son
More than in words?
Laertes   To cut his throat i'th' church.

[1] *what we wish to do*
[2] *slackening, loss of urgency*
[3] *the raw centre of the open sore*

Claudius continues. When Hamlet comes back, he will make sure that the Prince is reminded of Laertes' talent. Once Hamlet is sufficiently enthusiastic about the idea, the King will stage a fencing contest between the two of them. Although the rapiers supplied for the contest will all look similar, one of them will have a sharp, lethal point, unlike the others with the usual blunted end; this sharpened rapier is the one that Laertes will choose.

Laertes is enthusiastic. To be doubly sure of the efficacy of his rapier, he will dip its point in a deadly poison that he possesses: the slightest scratch will then result in Hamlet's death.

The King, eager to ensure that the plan does not fail and in some way reveal his intention, decides that a second line of attack is necessary. He will prepare a poisoned drink; even if Hamlet escapes wounding by Laertes' rapier, he is bound to call for refreshment after the heat and struggle of the fencing-match, and the King will make sure that he drinks from the poisoned cup.

The Queen now enters, bringing news of another dreadful misfortune. Ophelia has drowned. In her madness she was making garlands with the branches of a willow, the tree of sadness and lost love, tangling a profusion of wild flowers in its boughs. As she was climbing the tree, a branch overhanging the river gave way:

Queen   Her clothes spread wide,
And mermaid-like awhile they bore her up,
Which time she chanted snatches of old lauds,[1]
As one incapable[2] of her own distress,
Or like a creature native and indued
Unto that element.[3] But long it could not be
Till that her garments, heavy with their drink,
Pull'd the poor wretch from her melodious lay
To muddy death.

[1] *hymns*

[2] *unaware*

[3] *born to live in the water*

Unable to contain his grief at his sister's death, Laertes weeps inconsolably. He leaves, burning with anguish and indignation. The King, anxious to keep the young man's rage under control, follows him.

When writing of Ophelia's death, Shakespeare may well have recalled the drowning of a woman in the river Avon at Tiddington, near Stratford-on-Avon. It happened when he was fifteen years old, and aroused considerable public interest. There was great uncertainty as to whether her death was suicide or not, and it was two months before a verdict was reached: the coroner's jury eventually decided that she had not taken her own life.

If this incident did indeed come to Shakespeare's mind, perhaps it was prompted by a strange coincidence; the dead woman's name was Katherine Hamlet.

Some twenty-five years after Shakespeare's death, civil war between the English Parliament and the Crown was looming. The London theatres were temporarily closed; a couple of years later, the closure was declared permanent by the Puritanical revolutionary government. The Globe, where many of Shakespeare's plays had first been performed, was demolished, and the site used for housing.

It was to be fifteen years before theatrical performances were again legalised, with the Restoration of the monarchy in 1660. However, in the intervening years the performing arts had not died out altogether. Apart from private, often surreptitious performances of plays, the tradition of 'drolls' - brief sketches adapted from old plays, presented by travelling players at fairs and taverns - gained greatly in popularity. One of the most famous of these, adapted from *Hamlet*, was entitled *The Grave-Makers*.

A controversial verdict

V, i

Out in the graveyard, a grave-digger is about to prepare Ophelia's burial-place. He is engaged in earnest, albeit confused discussion with his companion on the question of suicide. There is some doubt in people's minds as to whether Ophelia died accidentally or took her own life; however, it has been officially agreed that she is entitled to the Christian burial normally denied to those who have committed suicide. The grave-digger is sceptical:

Grave-digger	Is she to be buried in Christian burial, when she wilfully seeks her own salvation?[1]
Companion	I tell thee she is, therefore make her grave straight. The crowner hath sat on her[2] and finds it Christian burial.
Grave-digger	How can that be, unless she drowned herself in her own defence?

[1] *more appropriately, 'damnation'; suicide was considered a mortal sin*
[2] *the coroner has held an inquest on her death*

The law on suicide is a complicated business, insists the grave-digger, and it involves subtle distinctions:

Grave-digger	Here lies the water - good. Here stands the man - good. If the man go to this water and drown himself, it is, will he nill he, he goes, mark you that. But if the water come to him and drown him, he drowns not himself. Argal,[1] he that is not guilty of his own death shortens not his own life.

[1] *ergo (therefore)*

His friend remains unconvinced. He is sure of one thing, however: the fact that the dead woman was a member of the nobility undoubtedly had an influence on the coroner's sympathetic verdict.

The grave-digger agrees, although as far as he is concerned the true aristocracy is made up of those who, like himself, share the ancient, original profession of digging the earth:

Grave-digger   . . . the more pity that
                        great folk should have countenance[1] in this world
                        to drown or hang themselves more than their
                        even-Christen.[2] Come, my spade. There is no
                        ancient gentlemen but gardeners, ditchers, and
                        grave-makers - they hold up Adam's profession.

                        [1] approval, endorsement
                        [2] fellow Christians

   With this, the grave-digger sets to work. He sends his friend
off to fetch a drink, and starts singing as he prepares the grave.

A pause for thought

Horatio has rejoined the Prince, and the two of them, on their
way to the castle, are passing through the graveyard. Hamlet, intrigued to hear the grave-digger singing in these surroundings,
stops for a moment.
   The grave-digger, busily clearing out his pit, tosses out a
skull, and Hamlet picks it up curiously. Perhaps it once be-
longed to a scheming politician, he reflects, or a courtier or aris-
tocrat; regardless of its status in life, though, it has ended up
suffering the indignity of a careless thump from a grave-digger's
spade.
   Hamlet decides to talk to the grave-digger, and asks the man
whose grave he is digging. It is his own, he replies unhelpfully;
he is the one who is digging it. Hamlet asks him how long he
has practised his profession. Although the grave-digger does not
recognise the Prince, he has some knowledge of royal matters,
and remembers the day that Hamlet's father slew the King of
Norway:

Grave-digger   . . . I came to't that day that our last King Hamlet
                 o'ercame Fortinbras.
Hamlet   How long is that since?
Grave-digger   Cannot you tell that? Every fool can tell that. It
                 was that very day that young Hamlet was born -
                 he that is mad and sent into England.

Fascinated, Hamlet tries to find out what the grave-digger
knows about his supposed madness, but the man's answers lead
him nowhere. He turns to the subject of the man's profession,
asking him how long a body might last before rotting away.
Eight or nine years at most, replies the grave-digger: but corpses
are not what they used to be, he complains, and these days many
are liable to putrefy as soon as they are in the ground.

The grave-digger picks another skull from the pit, remarking
that he knew its owner when he was alive, many years ago. It
comes as a shock to Hamlet when its identity is revealed, and his
boyhood memories come flooding back:

Grave-digger   A pestilence on him for a mad rogue! A poured a
                 flagon of Rhenish[1] on my head once. This same
                 skull, sir, was Yorick's skull, the King's jester.
Hamlet   This? [*Takes the skull.*]
Grave-digger   E'en that.
Hamlet   Alas, poor Yorick. I knew him, Horatio, a fellow
                 of infinite jest, of most excellent fancy.[2] He hath
                 bore me on his back a thousand times . . . Where
                 be your gibes[3] now, your gambols, your songs,
                 your flashes of merriment, that were wont to set
                 the table on a roar?

[1] *a jug of wine*
[2] *imagination, inventiveness*
[3] *taunts, teasing*

The idea of death as a universal leveller of humanity appeals greatly to Hamlet. He delights in the thought that a great conqueror may end up in the most mundane of situations, but his enthusiasm is not shared by his dispassionate friend:

Hamlet	To what base uses we may return, Horatio! Why, may not imagination trace the noble dust of Alexander till a find it stopping a bung-hole?[1]
Horatio	'Twere to consider too curiously[2] to consider so.

> [1] *used as a clay stopper to plug the hole in a beer-barrel*
> [2] *to think too ingeniously*

Hamlet and Laertes clash

Hamlet's amused contemplation is interrupted by the arrival of a funeral procession. He watches, unseen, as a coffin is carried towards the freshly-dug grave. Amongst the mourners are the King, the Queen, and Laertes. Hamlet is intrigued. This is clearly the burial of someone of high standing; yet the lack of the full funeral service suggests a death by suicide.

Laertes is angrily questioning the lack of ceremony. The priest, unmoved, insists that no more can be done. In fact, it was only under pressure from the King, he implies, that the Church has allowed her to be buried in consecrated ground. Laertes remains defiant:

Laertes	Lay her i'th' earth, And from her fair and unpolluted flesh May violets spring. I tell thee, churlish priest, A minist'ring angel shall my sister be When thou liest howling.

Hamlet is stunned as he suddenly realises the truth: the grave is for Ophelia. He watches in horror as her body, in its open coffin, is lowered into the ground. His mother scatters flowers sadly over the corpse:

Queen   Farewell.
    I hop'd thou shouldst have been my Hamlet's
      wife:
    I thought thy bride-bed to have deck'd,
      sweet maid,
    And not have strew'd thy grave.

Frantic with grief and anger, Laertes leaps into the grave to embrace his sister, crying out that he wishes to be buried alive alongside her. At this point, Hamlet announces his presence and approaches the grave. Without hesitation Laertes attacks him: as far as he is concerned, the Prince is responsible for his sister's death as well as his father's.

After a violent struggle, the two men are dragged apart, but Hamlet continues to taunt his opponent mercilessly: Laertes' love for Ophelia is as nothing compared to his own, he claims, and his protestations of grief are nothing more than noisy rhetoric. The King and Queen try to pacify Laertes, assuring him that Hamlet's madness is the cause of his cruel words.

> *"In this world of madness the only soil suitable for the 'rose of May' is the earth which covers her dead body. The flowers which the Queen drops into her grave mark the defeat of love and the end of hope in the play. The graveyard scene is one of the most tragic in the play because the characters are burying the future."*
>
> Nigel Alexander, *Poison, Play and Duel*, 1971

When Hamlet has left, Claudius takes Laertes aside and begs
him to be patient, reminding him of the planned fencing-match:

King   This grave shall have a living monument.[1]
                An hour of quiet[2] shortly shall we see;
                Till then in patience our proceeding be.

[1] *an eternal monument; perhaps in the form of the
sacrifice of another life*
[2] *time of peace*

"*One of the reasons for the interest generated by* Hamlet *is the
play's overriding preoccupation with what is hidden and secret.
Shakespeare's text concerns itself primarily with secrets, with
their function, inception, management, continuation and expo-
sure . . . the stress upon sexuality, espionage and inheritance in*
Hamlet *all point to a fascination with secrets and to questions
of political moment in the period.*"

M. T. Burnett, *Hamlet and Secrets*, 1994

An assassination attempt comes to light

V, ii

Hamlet tells Horatio of the events during his voyage to England, before his capture by the pirates who eventually returned him to Denmark. He was lying uneasily in his cabin, he recalls, kept awake by a nameless sense of anxiety and dread. He decided, on impulse, to steal up to the cabin of his escorts Rosencrantz and Guildenstern. In retrospect, he is glad of the hasty, unplanned action, which was to save his life. It has convinced him that there are forces at work in human affairs which cannot be foreseen or controlled even with the most thorough planning:

Hamlet   Our indiscretion sometime serves us well
When our deep plots do pall;[1] and that should learn us
There's a divinity that shapes our ends,[2]
Rough-hew them how we will . . .[3]

[1] *when our complex stratagems fail*
[2] *that governs our destinies*
[3] *regardless of our own crude attempts to determine our fates*

Once in his companions' cabin, Hamlet reports, he searched through their belongings, groping in the darkness for the letter which they were to deliver to the English King on arrival. Finding it, he returned to his cabin, broke open the royal seal, and read Claudius's orders. His sense of foreboding had not been unfounded:

Hamlet   . . . I found, Horatio -
              Ah, royal knavery! - an exact command,
              Larded[1] with many several sorts of reasons
              Importing Denmark's health, and England's too . . .
              That on the supervise, no leisure bated,[2]
              No, not to stay[3] the grinding of the axe,
              My head should be struck off.

> [1] *dressed, embellished*
> [2] *immediately following the reading of the letter, with
>   no time lost*
> [3] *allow time for*

Horatio can hardly believe what he is hearing; but Hamlet still has the letter in his possession, and hands it to his friend as proof of the King's intentions.

Returning to his account, Hamlet describes how he hurriedly forged a new letter for Rosencrantz and Guildenstern to deliver. Taking care to imitate the wordy diplomatic style of the original, he ensured that he would not be the one to meet a violent end in England. The forged letter, like the original, contained a royal command:

Hamlet   An earnest conjuration[1] from the King,
      As England[2] was his faithful tributary,
      As love between them like the palm might
        flourish . . .
      And many such-like 'as'es of great charge,
      That on the view and knowing of these contents,
      Without debatement further more or less,
      He should those bearers[3] put to sudden death,
      Not shriving-time allowed.[4]

> [1] *appeal*
> [2] *the King of England*
> [3] *those delivering the letter; Rosencrantz and*
> *Guildenstern*
> [4] *allowing no time for the confession and forgiveness*
> *of sins*

Sealing the letter with his father's ring, which contains the royal seal of Denmark, Hamlet then returned to his escorts' cabin and carefully placed the forged letter where he had found the original. Horatio cannot hide his dismay at the fate awaiting the two men. Hamlet angrily justifies his action, claiming that they deserve punishment for acting as the King's willing agents:

Horatio   So Guildenstern and Rosencrantz go to't.
Hamlet   Why, man, they did make love to this
       employment.
      They are not near my conscience, their defeat
      Does by their own insinuation[1] grow.

> [1] *involvement, connivance*

Retribution on the man who killed his father, and who has now tried to kill him, is of the utmost urgency. The King will soon hear of the death of Hamlet's two escorts, and his suspicions will be aroused; in the meantime, Hamlet must act swiftly.

In his renewed passion for revenge, Hamlet sympathises with the plight of Laertes. He regrets having taunted him so cruelly at Ophelia's graveside, and resolves to win back his friendship.

> *"Hamlet is the permanent rebel . . . and would be the same in any society or period of history. He works out his morality as he goes along, taking nothing on trust, and approaches life like an actor, always trying on new characterisations to see if they fit."*
>
> Laurence Olivier, speaking at the inaugural production of *Hamlet* at the National Theatre, 1963

A competition is staged

Osric, a courtier, comes to greet Hamlet. The King has sent him, he explains: but Hamlet's mocking of his deferential manner and courtly language throw him into confusion, and he makes slow headway with his message. The King's request concerns Laertes, says Osric, and his extravagant praise is parodied in Hamlet's reply:

Osric	Sir, here is newly come to court Laertes - believe me, an absolute gentleman, full of most excellent differences,[1] of very soft society[2] and great showing. Indeed, to speak feelingly of him, he is the card or calendar of gentry . . .
Hamlet	Sir, his definement suffers no perdition in you, though I know to divide him inventorially would dozy th'arithmetic of memory . . .[3]

[1] *distinction*

[2] *agreeable manners*

[3] *to recite a list of all his good qualities would be a daunting feat of memory*

Eventually Osric manages to communicate his news: the King has placed a wager on a fencing-match between Laertes and Hamlet. Claudius has staked six prize horses on the contest, while Laertes is offering six fine French rapiers. If Laertes succeeds in beating Hamlet by more than three hits in twelve bouts, he wins the wager. If Hamlet is willing, says Osric, the contest can take place right away. Hamlet agrees, and sends Osric back to the King to pass on his acceptance of the challenge.

A few minutes later, another courtier comes to see whether Hamlet is ready for the contest: he replies that he is. The courtier mentions that the Queen has asked Hamlet to treat Laertes with special courtesy before the match, perhaps fearing that the fighting could become too heated after the angry encounter at the graveside.

Horatio feels that his friend's chances against the skilful Laertes are poor. Hamlet insists that he is in good form, although he admits to a sudden, strange sense of disquiet, even fear, that he cannot explain.

Horatio urges him to call off the match if anything is troubling him, but Hamlet refuses to be swayed by his premonition.

In fact, he feels strangely calm and fatalistic, and speaks as if he were facing death rather than a sporting contest:

Horatio	If your mind dislike anything, obey it. I will forestall their repair[1] hither and say you are not fit.
Hamlet	Not a whit. We defy augury.[2] There is special providence in the fall of a sparrow.[3] If it be now, 'tis not to come; if it be not to come, it will be now; if it be not now, yet it will come. The readiness is all.

[1] *arrival, gathering*
[2] *premonitions, omens*
[3] *even the life span of a sparrow is governed by God's will*

A trumpet sounds, and a procession now sweeps in to join Hamlet and Horatio: the King and Queen, with their courtiers, followers and servants; Laertes, with attendants carrying the foils for the fencing-match; officers with trumpets and drums; and servants arranging tables, furnishings and cushions.

The scene is set for the contest. Hamlet and Laertes take centre stage.

"... it is a vulgar and barbarous play, and would not be tolerated by the lowest public of France or Italy. Hamlet goes mad in the second act, and his mistress in the third; the Prince kills his mistress's father, imagining he is killing a rat, and the heroine throws herself into the river. Her grave is dug on the stage; the grave-diggers utter dubious pleasantries worthy of their status, whilst holding skulls in their hands; Prince Hamlet replies to their abominable vulgarities with idiocies no less disgusting. Meanwhile, one of the characters conquers Poland . . . One would imagine this piece to be the work of a drunken savage . . . and yet there are to be found in Hamlet, unaccountably, some sublime passages worthy of the greatest genius."

Voltaire, *Dissertation sur la Tragédie*, 1752

The plotting ends in catastrophe

Claudius starts the proceedings by bringing the two contestants together and calling upon them to shake hands. Hamlet then gives a public apology for the killing of Laertes' father: it was done in a fit of madness, he says, a madness which is as much an enemy to the true Hamlet as it is to Laertes. He appeals to his opponent to think of him as a brother, not a foe.

Laertes' reply is cautious and reserved. He accepts Hamlet's apology, but revenge for his father's murder is a duty which he cannot disregard. It is a question he intends to discuss with some elder advisers, experienced in matters of honour: in the meantime, Hamlet's offer of goodwill is welcome.

Hamlet calls for the foils, the specially-blunted rapiers used in sporting contests. He jokes about his own lack of skill at fencing:

Hamlet	I'll be your foil,[1] Laertes. In mine ignorance Your skill shall like a star i'th' darkest night Stick fiery off[2] indeed.

[1] *the setting of a jewel, designed to highlight its brilliance*
[2] *stand out brightly*

The competitors choose their foils. Laertes takes care to select the sharpened, poisoned weapon which, with the King's connivance, he has prepared in advance. Hamlet takes a foil and, with a wry warning to the King that he has placed his bet on the wrong man, prepares to play.

Servants now enter carrying flagons of wine. Claudius announces that he will drink a toast if Hamlet scores the first hit, and will command the drums to be struck: the trumpets will then sound, in turn, and the cannons out on the castle battlements will be fired in celebration. As a special sign of honour to the Prince, Claudius will dissolve a priceless pearl in the cup as he drinks to his nephew's health.

The contest begins, and the two men fence energetically. Hamlet, unaware of his opponent's deadly weapon, claims the first hit. Laertes disagrees, but is overruled, and the King raises his cup:

Hamlet	One.
Laertes	No.
Hamlet	Judgment.
Osric	A hit, a very palpable hit.
Laertes	Well, again.
King	Stay, give me drink. Hamlet this pearl is thine. Here's to thy health.

As the drums and trumpets sound, and the cannon outside thunder, Claudius crushes the pearl into his wine. He does not drink, though, handing the cup instead to Hamlet. Keen to continue with the fencing, Hamlet puts the drink aside.

The second bout begins. Again Hamlet manages to score a hit against his rival. He is becoming breathless and sweaty: Gertrude is concerned, and gives him her handkerchief so that he can dry himself. She drinks a toast to him in encouragement.

Claudius watches in horror as Gertrude lifts the cup. It is the drink that he passed to Hamlet a moment ago, and has been laced with poison. Unable to reveal the truth in public, he tries to dissuade Gertrude: but she insists, drinking from the cup and passing it to her son. Yet again, Hamlet refuses to drink. He is eager to play the third bout. His mother holds him back for a moment as she fondly dabs the sweat from his face.

Laertes has a private word with the King: now is the time for the fatal blow, he believes. Claudius, his plan already hideously awry, cannot give his consent. Laertes himself is starting to have doubts:

Laertes	My lord, I'll hit him now.
King	I do not think't.
Laertes	[*aside*] And yet it is almost against my conscience.
Hamlet	Come for the third, Laertes. You do but dally. I pray you pass[1] with your best violence. I am afeard you make a wanton of me.[2]

[1] *attack, thrust*
[2] *let me win, like a spoilt child*

Stung by Hamlet's teasing, Laertes becomes more aggressive. The third bout is declared equal, with no hit to either party: but at this point Laertes lunges unexpectedly at his opponent, drawing blood. The two men scuffle violently. The King calls desperately for them to part, but Hamlet ignores him. In the struggle he has snatched the sharpened rapier, and now he strikes angrily at Laertes, wounding him in return.

The Queen collapses, and the panic intensifies. The King tries desperately to reassure the court that she has merely fainted at the sight of blood. In her dying words, though, she manages to gasp out the truth: the drink intended for Hamlet has poisoned her.

In the ensuing uproar, Hamlet cries out for the culprits to be found. They are already present, reveals Laertes, and it is not only his mother who is the victim of treachery:

Hamlet	O villainy! Ho! Let the door be lock'd.
	Treachery! Seek it out.
Laertes	It is here, Hamlet. Hamlet, thou art slain.
	No medicine in the world can do thee good;
	In thee there is not half an hour's life.
	The treacherous instrument is in thy hand,
	Unbated and envenom'd.[1] The foul practice
	Hath turn'd itself on me. Lo, here I lie,
	Never to rise again. Thy mother's poison'd.
	I can no more. The King - the King's to blame.

[1] *sharpened and poisoned*

Hamlet looks in horror at the rapier that he has just snatched from his opponent. It has given Laertes his revenge; now Hamlet will have his, before it is too late. The onlookers cry out in terror as he stabs the King with the poisoned blade. The King's cries for help are cut short as Hamlet pours the remainder of the poisoned wine down his throat.

Hamlet puts his trust in Horatio

The sight of the dying King gives Laertes no cause for sorrow. Dying himself, he reflects that Claudius deserves his fate. He asks Hamlet's forgiveness, offers his own, and, with the hope that they will both be shown mercy in the next world, he dies.

> "*The evil in the world is not the product of the specially cor-*
> *rupt present generation, it has its roots in the generations that*
> *went before and also were corrupt . . . what excites Shakespeare*
> *in this play is the impossibility of conceiving an action which*
> *could justly be termed virtuous, in view of the basis of original*
> *sin.*"
>
> Rebecca West, *The Court and the Castle*, 1957

Hamlet too is now starting to suffer the deadly effects of the poisoned rapier. He asks his faithful friend Horatio to tell the world the truth about his father's murder and the dreadful events that have sprung from it:

Hamlet   You that look pale and tremble at this chance,[1]
                That are but mutes[2] or audience to this act,
                Had I but time - as this fell[3] sergeant, Death,
                Is strict in his arrest - O, I could tell you -
                But let it be. Horatio, I am dead,
                Thou livest. Report me and my cause aright . . .

                [1] *misfortune*
                [2] *actors looking on, with no lines to speak*
                [3] *terrible, ruthless*

Horatio refuses: he wishes to die with his friend, and he grabs the cup of poisoned wine, determined to drink the few remaining drops. Hamlet manages to pull the cup from his grasp, and again beseeches him to make the truth known:

Hamlet   O God, Horatio, what a wounded name,
                Things standing thus unknown, shall I leave
                    behind me.

If thou didst ever hold me in thy heart,
Absent thee from felicity[1] awhile,
And in this harsh world draw thy breath in pain
To tell my story.

[1] *the contentment of death*

Suddenly a volley of shots rings out from outside the castle. A courtier comes in to report that Fortinbras is nearby. Returning in triumph from Poland, he has encountered the ambassadors sent from England, and is firing a fusillade in greeting. All are now on their way to the castle.

As he dies, Hamlet appeals for the throne of Denmark, which was to have been his, to go to the Norwegian Prince. There is no time to say more. There are no more words:

Hamlet	. . . I do prophesy th'election lights[1]
	On Fortinbras. He has my dying voice.
	So tell him, with th'occurrents more and less
	Which have solicited[2] - the rest is silence.
Horatio	Now cracks a noble heart. Good night, sweet prince,
	And flights of angels sing thee to thy rest.

[1] *will settle, will fall*
[2] *the events, great and small, which have persuaded me*

"*Hamlet falls apart in the space between himself and his actions . . .*"

Terry Eagleton, *William Shakespeare*, 1986

Fortinbras reclaims his kingdom

Fortinbras, accompanied by his officers, now enters: so too do the
ambassadors from England. A scene of carnage greets them.
Hamlet, his mother, Claudius and Laertes are all dead. Fortinbras
looks on in dismay:

Fortinbras   O proud Death,
                What feast is toward[1] in thine eternal cell,
                That thou so many princes at a shot
                So bloodily hast struck?

        [1] *being prepared*

One of the ambassadors reveals that the King's order has been
carried out, and yet more names are added to the roll of the dead:

Ambassador   The ears are senseless that should give us hearing
                To tell him his commandment is fulfill'd,
                That Rosencrantz and Guildenstern are dead.

That was not the King's command, declares Horatio. Of this,
and of many other events, he has much to impart. Things that
have remained hidden must be brought to light:

Horatio   So shall you hear
                Of carnal, bloody, and unnatural acts,
                Of accidental judgments, casual slaughters,
                Of deaths put on[1] by cunning and forc'd cause,[2]
                And, in this upshot, purposes mistook
                Fall'n on th'inventors' heads. All this can I
                Truly deliver.

        [1] *brought about, instigated*
        [2] *contrivance*

The events that have led to the present scene of slaughter must quickly be made public, urges Horatio. If they are not, the cycle of deceit, treachery and bloodshed is liable to continue. Even the bodies themselves must be put on display.

Fortinbras agrees. The whole Danish court, he assures Horatio, will be assembled shortly to hear the truth.

The King and his successor are dead. Fortinbras, with his army, is now effectively in control of Elsinore. He believes his family has ancient rights of ownership in Denmark; and Horatio confirms that Hamlet has nominated him as his chosen successor to the throne.

Fortinbras takes command. Hamlet would have proved a noble ruler had he lived, he announces: a warrior himself, he decrees that the Prince's funeral will be performed with full military honours. He orders his officers to carry the bodies away. Outside, the cannons roar in commemoration of the dead.

ACKNOWLEDGEMENTS

The following publications have proved invaluable as sources of factual information and critical insight:

Nigel Alexander, *Poison, Play and Duel: A Study in Hamlet*, Routledge and Kegan Paul, 1971

Charles Boyce, *Shakespeare A to Z*, Roundtable Press, 1990

Mark Thornton Burnett, *Hamlet and Secrets*, in *New Essays on Hamlet*, edited by M. T. Burnett and J. Manning, AMS Press, 1994

Terry Eagleton, *William Shakespeare*, Blackwell, 1986

Levi Fox, *The Shakespeare Handbook*, Bodley Head, 1987

G. B. Harrison, *Introducing Shakespeare*, Pelican, 1966

Harold Jenkins, Introduction to the Arden edition of *Hamlet*, Methuen, 1982

Jan Kott, *Shakespeare Our Contemporary*, Doubleday, 1965

François Laroque, *Shakespeare: Court, Crowd and Playhouse*, Gallimard, 1991

D. H. Lawrence, *Twilight in Italy*, Duckworth, 1913

Maynard Mack, *Everybody's Shakespeare*, Bison Books, 1993

John Masefield, *William Shakespeare*, Thornton Butterworth, 1911

Robert Speaight, *Shakespeare: The Man and his Achievement*, Dent, 1977

Caroline Spurgeon, *Shakespeare's Imagery and What It Tells Us*, Cambridge University Press, 1935

Kay Stanton, *Hamlet's Whores*, in *New Essays on Hamlet*, edited by M. T. Burnett and J. Manning, AMS Press, 1994

Joseph C. Tardiff, *Shakespearean Criticism*, Gale Research Inc., 1993

Peter Thomson, *Shakespeare's Professional Career*, Cambridge University Press, 1992

Stanley Wells, General Introduction to *William Shakespeare: The Complete Works*, Oxford University Press, 1988

Rebecca West, *The Court and the Castle: Some Treatments of a Recurrent Theme*, Yale University Press, 1957

Charles Williams and Edmund Chambers, *A Short Life of Shakespeare*, Oxford University Press, 1933

All quotations from *Hamlet* are taken from the Arden Shakespeare.